Ellen Emma Guthrie

Old Scottish Customs

Local and General

Ellen Emma Guthrie

Old Scottish Customs
Local and General

ISBN/EAN: 9783337243401

Printed in Europe, USA, Canada, Australia, Japan

Cover: Foto ©Suzi / pixelio.de

More available books at **www.hansebooks.com**

OLD SCOTTISH CUSTOMS

LOCAL AND GENERAL

BY

E. J. GUTHRIE

Author of "Tales of the Jacobites," etc.

LONDON: HAMILTON, ADAMS & CO.
GLASGOW: THOMAS D. MORISON.
1885

PREFACE.

IN placing before the reading public this small book on a great subject, it may be desirable to give a few words of explanation regarding its compilation. Some fifteen or sixteen years ago, in connection with other literary work regarding parochial and local matters throughout Scotland, the writer had occasion to consult somewhat fully, many of the works on such subjects,—namely, works regarding topographical history and description. In these volumes, mostly either large, rare, or expensive and difficult of access by the general public, numerous references, it was observed, were made to old customs of all sorts, now either quite obsolete or rapidly becoming so.

Getting increasingly interested in these frequent references, jottings were taken in many instances. Since then the accumulation has been added to from time to time, and from many sources,—by personal contact with the people and otherwise,—and now there being a goodly number, it has been suggested that they would form an interesting little volume, which might not be altogether unacceptable to those fellow-countrymen who are interested in the manners and customs of our fathers. In the circumstances described, the result of the protracted but pleasing process of research, sadly imperfect as it may be, is laid before the public in all humbleness of spirit, and as such it is hoped that criticism may be withheld. As the customs themselves only are given, and, not being burdened with remark or comment, the style of the collection must necessarily be fragmentary and brief; perhaps however, this latter feature, in these days of the making of many books, may not be altogether a disadvantage.

With regard to the works already referred to, as the source from which the writer is indebted for most of the various customs described in these pages. Almost all authoritative and standard authors likely to be of assistance have been consulted. Among many others the following may be specified:—Skene's *The Highlanders of Scotland*, 2 vols.; Chalmers's *Caledonia*, 3 vols., 4to.; Martin's *Description of the Western Islands;* Pennant's *Tour in Scotland*, 3 vols.; Johnson and Boswell's *Tour in Scotland;* Roger's *Scotland Social and Domestic*, and other writings; Sir Walter Scott's various writings; Chambers' *Picture of Scotland*, and other writings; Forsyth's *Beauties of Scotland*, 5 vols.; Miss Gordon Cumming's *In the Hebrides*, etc., etc. But chief of all, is the magnificent collection edited by Sir John Sinclair entitled the *Statistical Account of Scotland*, in 21 volumes, and written by the respective parish ministers. The value and interest attaching to these latter volumes is far beyond all ordinary estimate, and yet the work is not at all easy of access, and is seldom seen by the general reader.

London, May, 1885.

CONTENTS.

CHAPTER I.

Introductory—The Beltane Customs—Origin of many Scottish Customs to a great extent unknown—Holy-wells—Water Spirits—The Father of Northern Magic—Fancy's Land—The Study of Old Customs, ... 13

CHAPTER II.

The Curfew—Curious Foot Ball Custom at Coldingham—Hand Ball—Rural Festival at Lochtie—Old Scottish Funeral Customs — Burgess Customs at Selkirk — Customs at Forfar commemorative of Queen Margaret—Charitable Feast at Kirkmichael—Singular Custom at South Queensferry—The Burry Man, ... 24

CHAPTER III.

Women playing at foot ball—Singular wedding custom in Ayrshire and the Border—The ancient game of golf—Unpleasant Burgess custom at Edinburgh—The Robin Hood games—The Poor Folks in Edinburgh—The Siller Square—Customs in connection with the Blue Blanket banner—The old custom of Handfasting, ... 36

CHAPTER IV.

The Herds' Festival at Midlothian—Old customs in connection with Archery—The Hangman's Right at Dumfries—The Cure for Scolds at Langholm—Customs regarding Holy wells—Curious customs at Rutherglen—The feast of Sour Cakes—Riding the Marches—Foot-Race at Biggar—Riding the Stang, ... 49

CHAPTER V.

Old Marriage Customs in Perthshire—Superstitions regarding the cure of disease—Scottish customs regarding the observance of Hallow e'en—General description of this festival—Pulling the Green Kail—Eating the Apple—Burning Nuts—Sowing Hemp Seed—Winnowing Corn—Measuring the Bean Stack—Eating the Herring—Dipping the Shirt Sleeve—The Three Plates—Throwing the Clue—Illustrative Anecdote—Pricking the Egg—The Summons of Death, . . . 63

CHAPTER VI.

Carters' Plays at Liberton—Superstitions in connection with St. Catherine's Well—Old customs at Musselburgh—Riding the Marches again—Lanark and Linlithgow—The Polwarth Thorn—Gretna Green Marriages—Curious Land Tenure Customs—Traditions regarding Macduff's Cross—Singular customs regarding Licensed Beggars in Scotland, . 76

CHAPTER VII.

Customs connected with St. Filan's Well—Scottish Custom regarding May Dew—St. Serf's festival at Culross—Palm Sunday held at Lanark—Riding the Marches at Lanark—Killing a Sheep at Lanark Old Custom at Kelso—The King's Ease at Ayr—Burning the Chaff after death—Creeling the Bridegroom in Berwickshire—Marriage customs and Superstitions in Invernesshire—Ancient customs at Carluke—Scottish funeral customs—Horse-Racing in Scotland—Farmer's Parade in Ayrshire—Shooting for the Siller Gun at Dumfries, . . 88

CHAPTER VIII.

Interesting Hand-ball custom in Perthshire—Old custom in connection with Scottish Coronations—The Game of Shinty at Roseneath—Playing Football on Sunday—Christmas Sports in Aberdeenshire—Festive Games at Cullen—Marriage and Funeral Customs at Knockando—Superstitious customs in connection with the Dhu Loch—The Well of Lorretta at Musselburgh—Chapman's Festival at Preston—Cock-fighting at Westruther—The Wapinshaw at Perth—Horse-racing at Perth in Olden Times—The Mount of Peace—Holy-wells at Muthill, . - 103

CHAPTER IX.

Marriage and Funeral customs at Pettie—The Duke of Perth and the Crieff Fair—Fairy doings in Inverness-shire—Curious marriage custom at Ardersier—Superstitious customs at Foderty—The old Scottish game of curling—Farmers' custom at Elgin—Happy and unhappy feet—Funeral customs at Campsie—Gool Riding in Perthshire, . . 119

CHAPTER X.

Old Customs at Kirkmichael—The Pedlar's Tournament at Leslie—Superstitious custom at St. Monance—The Touch Hills—The Maiden Feast in Perthshire—The Society of Chapmen at Dunkeld—Announcement of Death at Hawick—The customs in connection with Nicknames—Religious custom on the approach of Death—Riding the Marches at Hawick—Scottish Masonic customs—Candlemas customs, ... 127

CHAPTER XI.

Strange Custom at Kirkmaiden—Singular obituary announcement at Bo'ness—Holy-well observances in Kincardineshire—Ancient races at Kilmarnock—Creeling the Bridegroom again—Old Border customs—Alarm signals—The right hand unbaptised—The fiery peat—Good faith of the Borderers—Sunday dissipation—Punishment of matrimonial infidelity in former times—Riding the stang—Marriage processions—Odd football custom at Foulden—Strange holy well superstitions—Curious customs with regard to fishing—The siller gun of Kirkcudbright, ... 139

CHAPTER XII.

Old Lammastide customs at Midlothian—Some Galloway customs—Throwing the hoshen—Fykes Fair—Giving up the names—Old games—The priest's cat—Customs at new moon—Old marriage ceremonies—Bar for bar—The game of Blinchamps—The game of Burly Whush—The game of king and queen of Cantalon, ... 151

CHAPTER XIII.

Superstitious customs with regard to good or bad omens—Yule boys—The rumbling well in Galloway—Marrying days in Galloway—Michaelmas custom in Argyleshire—Saint Cowie and Saint Couslan—The lucky well of Beothaig—The bridge of one hair in Kincardineshire—The old custom of Rig and Rennel—Some old customs of the Sinclairs, 161

CHAPTER XIV.

Some old customs at Wick—Funeral processions at North Uist—Marriage customs among the poorer classes in the North—Going a rocking—Old customs in the Orkney Islands—Fisherman's customs in setting out for the fishing ground—The sow's day—St. Peter's day—Dingwall Court of Justice—Old custom at Eriska—Singular fisherman's custom at Fladda—Interesting Highland custom—Old customs at the Island of Eigg, . . . 171

CHAPTER XV.

Interesting customs at St. Kilda—The water-cross at Barra—Ocean Meat—Curious wooing custom in the Western Islands—Annual Festival in honour of St. Barr—The fiery circle—Old customs in the Island of Lewis — Singular cure for Scrofula — Strange custom regarding forced fire—Devotion to St. Flannan — Salmon-fishing Superstition — The Sea-god Shoney—Burying custom at Taransay—Michaelmas custom at Lingay—Customs regarding fowling expeditions, ... 179

CHAPTER XVI.

Form of prayer used for blessing a ship in the Western Islands—Dedicating horses to the sun at Iona—Curious harvest custom in Island of Skye—Drinking Custom in the Clan Macleod—Old customs in connection with a holy loch in Skye—The Evil Eye in the Western Islands—Signalling customs in olden times—Evening amusements in the Western Islands in former times—Curious belief regarding quarreling and Herrings—Belief in Brownies in the Western Islands, ... 190

CHAPTER XVII.

Some interesting customs and superstitions in Shetland—Observance of Yule-tide—Strange funeral custom—The water of health—The healing thread — Curing ringworm — Curing burns — Elf-shot — Wearing charms—Singular calving custom—Belief in fairies—The doings of fairies—The high land of the trows—Superstition regarding neighbour's profits, ... 198

CHAPTER XVIII.

Some old Highland customs—Courtship in former times—Marriage ceremonies—Manner of inviting guests—The bridegroom and the bride—The procession—Winning the kail—The Marriage feast—The dance — Funeral customs — Laying out the corpse—The lyke-wake—The coronach—The fiery cross—A Fasten's Eve custom—Some Lowland and general customs—Penal statutes at Galashiels—Peebles to the play—Marriage and kirking customs again—Family spirits or demons, . . . 206

CHAPTER XIX.

Holding Kate Kennedy's Day at St. Andrews—Golf again—Amusing account of its origin and history—Holy well customs at Dunkeld—Holy wells at Huntly—Numerous holy wells over Scotland—Superstitious customs connected therewith—The burning of the Clavie at Burghead, . . 218

CHAPTER XX.

Description of some of the old Druidical customs and their remains—The Ancient Gods of the Britons—The manner of celebrating the Bel-tein—The first day in May—The Relics of Druidical Worship in Kincardineshire—The day of Baal's fire—The day of the Fire of Peace—Druidical Sacrifices—May and Hallowe'en observances of Druidical origin—Tinto Hill in Lanarkshire—Remains of Druidical customs at Mouline—In Perthshire—At Cambuslang—Passing children and cattle through the fire, 225

OLD SCOTTISH CUSTOMS.

LOCAL AND GENERAL.

CHAPTER I.

Introductory — The Beltane Customs — Origin of many Scottish Customs to a great extent unknown — Holy-wells — Water Spirits — The Father of Northern Magic — Fancy's Land — The Study of Old Customs.

WITH the lapse of time many of our national and local customs which for so long a period, retained a firm and apparently lasting hold on the affections of the Scottish peasantry, have fallen into unmerited neglect. A similar fate has also overtaken those superstitious rites and observances so closely interwoven with our early national life—so tenaciously adhered to by our rude forefathers, even when the pure light of Christianity had dawned upon our northern shores, and still clung to when the gentle St. Ninian was proclaiming his glorious message amidst the wilds of Galloway, and when

Columba and his disciples had planted the cross, where for centuries had stood the proud monoliths of Paganism on the sea-girt isle of Iona.

Fortunately for those who are desirous of enlightenment, on the subject of our ancient Scottish manners and customs; even in this so styled "restlessly progressive age," Scotland has her students of antiquities, who by their unwearied labours in the rich fields of antiquarian research, have obtained for us most valuable information in regard to these and other curious and interesting facts connected with our past history as a people. Our learned and devoted antiquaries have, as it were, taken up the glass of time and turned it backward with reverend hands to the dim twilight of history, restoring to us much that had seemed for ever lost, or that had been rendered unreal and shadowy by the mists of successive generations.

Thus, across the centuries that lie between, we seem to see the lurid Baal fires blazing from the summits of our mountain peaks, the commemorative Beltane customs, with their attendant mysteries. The countless pilgrimages made to our reputed holy and life-giving wells; and the dwellers on lone Orcadian shores, invoking the spirit of the storm, and offering up sacrifices to their heathen deities.

It is much to be regretted that while our older local customs and superstitions, connected with these very early and later times, have carefully been taken note of, in the generality of cases little account of their supposed origin has been given us. In all probability such was unknown to the actors themselves, and the bakers of the "dumb cakes" at Rutherglen, in common with the herdsmen and shepherds who kindled their fire and drank their *caudle* on Beltane day, were ignorant of the real nature of the mysterious practices in which they were engaged. In the words of Miss Gordon Cumming, "Though the old customs are still retained, their original meaning is entirely forgotten; and the man who throws a live peat after a woman about to increase the population, and he who on Hallowe'en throws a lighted brand over one shoulder without looking at whom he aims, little dreams whence sprang these time-honoured incidents."

The Beltane or Bel-tein (*Bel*, in Gaelic, signifies sun; and *tein*, fire) customs are believed to have had their origin in those heathen times, when our ancestors worshipped Baal the Sun god, and Ashtoreth,

"Astarte, queen of heaven,"

with certain mystic observances chiefly connected with fire. In druidical times four great fire-festivals were held at different periods of the year; namely, on the eve of May day, or Spring; on Midsummer's eve; on Hallowe'en, hence our Hallowe'en bonfires; and at Yule, the mid-winter feast.

The eve of May day still retains its name of Beltane or Beltein, and formerly, as we have already observed, it was a day set apart by the herdsmen and others of the Scottish peasantry, for the celebration of such time-honoured observances as were deemed suitable to the occasion, such as digging a hole on a hill top and lighting a fire therein; then lots are cast, and he on whom the lot falls, must leap seven times over the fire, while the young folks dance round in a circle. Then they cook their eggs and cakes, and all sit down to eat and drink and rise up to play.

Water as well as fire was anciently held in

great reverence by our druidical ancestors, and the homage paid to wells and springs in great measure owed its origin to the worship of Neith or Nait, the goddess of waters. Pennant, when in Skye found traces of four temples erected in memory of this popular deity.

There were numerous Holy wells in the Highlands and Lowlands of Scotland, which were much resorted to in cases of sickness by the more superstitious of the peasantry, and even yet in certain remote districts the old superstition still lingers. The benefits supposed to be derived from draughts of the sparkling waters varied in character. Certain fountains proved efficacious when the eye-sight was affected; others such as St. Fillans and Strathill, Perthshire, were resorted to in cases of insanity; a spring near Ayr cured King Robert Bruce of his leprosy; that of *Tobar-na-danhernid* was believed to denote whether a sick person would overcome his complaint; one loch in Ross-shire is said to cure deafness, and so on. Water drawn from under a bridge "o'er which the living walked and the dead were carried," as well as south-running water, were reputed to possess wonderful properties. Those pilgrims who frequented wells for healing purposes, made votive offerings to the guardian spirit of the water, or to the saints to whom they were dedicated. These generally consisted of pieces of cloth, thread, and other such simple materials —occasionally a small coin was deposited in the fountain. If trees and bushes grew in the immediate neighbourhood of these Siloams, to the branches of these the gifts were attached.

Well worship in common with witchcraft and sorcery was sternly prohibited in some instances by the early fathers of the Church. In A.D. 1182, St. Anselm in England forbade the superstitious practice, and so late as 1638 the General Assembly of Scotland waged a determined warfare against it and other idolatrous observances, as instanced by the following:—persons "found superstitiously to have passed in pilgrimage to Christ's Well (near Doune, Perthshire) on the Sundays of May to seek their health, that they shall repent in sacco (sackcloth) and linen three several Sabbaths, and pay twenty lib. (Pounds Scots) *toties quoties* for ilk fault." In 1652, the Kirk-Session of Auchterhouse dealt with a woman for carrying her child to a well in May.

The old superstitions once so common in the Orkney and Shetland Islands have in a great measure disappeared, but formerly the belief in witchcraft was almost universal, instances have occurred even at the end of last century. Hill spirits, kirk spirits, and water spirits, were held responsible for sickness and divers other misfortunes. " Trows " inhabited *Trolhouland*—the hill of demons or Trows—and within its recesses had their abodes, whose walls were dazzling with gold and silver. Brownies were the inmates of houses, and at night had tables placed for them in the barn where they slept, covered with bread, butter, cheese, and ale, while charms for killing sparrows that destroyed the early corn, expelling rats and mice from houses, for success in brewing and churning, procuring good luck, curing diseases of cattle and human beings, were in constant use. These and other superstitious beliefs, says a local writer, have been imported into Shetland in very early times. The same writer also tells us that these can be traced to the earliest period of our history, and that nowhere else in Scotland, excepting the remoter Hebrides, have they maintained their ground so long as in the popular creed of Shetland. This author styles Odin the preceptor if not the father of northern magic, and thinks that it was the early connexion of Orkney and Shetland with Scandinavia, and the belief in Odin which made the ancient inhabitants acquainted with the arts and mysteries embodied in the wild mythology of the northern peoples.

This once dread Odin—the Scandinavian sun-god—seems to have been a great magician. He instructed his subjects in the charms which rendered their weapons invincible in battle. He had two familiar spirits in the shape of ravens who sat on his shoulder and informed him of everything that went on in the outer world. These ravens, in the superstitious belief of the people, appear to have survived the days of paganism, and have figured in our trials for witchcraft during last century. Odin had also his messengers or handmaidens, the valkyries, who travelled through the air and over seas mounted on swift winged horses, with drawn swords, in order to select the particular mortals destined to die in battle, and to conduct them to Valhalla, the paradise of warriors. Odin is supposed to have stated that he knew a song of such marvellous power, that were he caught in a storm he could hush the winds and make the air perfectly calm.

An oath by Odin was formerly deemed legal as well as sacred. In some parts of Orkney it was the custom for all young couples meditating matrimony to go by moonlight to the Standing Stones of Stenness, known as the Temple of Odin, whom the woman, kneeling on the ground, must invoke. The lovers afterwards plighted their troth by clasping hands through the perforated stone of Odin. In the course of last century the elders of the local church punished a faithless lover because he had broken the promise thus made.

Notwithstanding all that has been written and said against our once popular beliefs, and in spite of "the ban of kirk and school,"

> "There's something in that ancient superstition,
> Which, erring as it is, our fancy loves,"

and the superstitions connected with our Highlands and Islands have found favour with the poet as well as furnished fertile fields for antiquarian discussion.

Who knows not Collins' beautiful lines :—

" 'Tis Fancy's land to which thou sett'st thy feet,
Where still, 'tis said, the fairy people meet
Beneath each birken shade on mead or hill.
There each trim lass that skims the milky store
To the swart tribes their creamy bowl allots ;
By night they sip it round the cottage door,
While airy minstrels warble jocund notes.
There every herd by sad experience knows
How wing'd with fate their elf-shot arrows fly
When the sick ewe her summer food foregoes,
Or, stretched on earth, the heart-smote heifers lie.
Such airy beings awe the untutored swain.

'Tis thine to sing how, framing hideous spells,
In Skye's lone isle the gifted wizard seer
Lodged in the wintry cave which Fate's fell spear,
Or in the depth of Unst's dark forest dwells.
How they whose sight such dreamy dreams engross,
With their own visions oft astonished droop
When o'er the watery strath or quaggy moss
They see the gliding ghosts unbodied troop ;
Or, if in sport, or on the festive green,
Their destined glance some gifted youth descry
Who now perhaps in lusty vigour seen
And rosy health, shall soon lamented die.
For them the viewless forms of air obey,
Their bidding heed, and at their beck repair ;
They know what spirit brews the stormful day,
And heartless oft like moody madness stare
To see the phantom trains their secret work prepare.
These filled in olden time the historic page,
When Shakespeare's self, with ivy-garland crowned,
Flew to these fairy climes, his fancy sheen

In musing hour; his wayward sisters found,
And with their terrors dressed the magic scene.
From them he sung when 'mid his bold design
Before the soul afflicted and aghast
The shadowy Kings of Banquo's fated line
Through the dark cave in gleamy pageant passed.

Yet frequent now at midnight's solemn hour
The rifted mounds their yawning cells unfold
And forth the monarchs stalk with sovereign power,
In pageant robes and wreathed with sheeny gold,
And on their twilight tombs aërial council hold."

Dean Ramsay has left a charming and truthful record of old Scottish life and manners, chiefly in the upper classes of society and derived from accessible sources; but the student of history or of antiquities who wishes to obtain an insight into our traditions and superstitions, as well as the local customs and usages of humble life, has an exceedingly wide and varied field for investigation, and abundance of encouragement to prosecute the search. A search regarding which, it may be said, little more than a beginning has been made, much that as yet is but imperfectly understood will be fully explained at some future time.

From personal acquaintance with Scottish social life, and by consulting numerous literary authorities, the editor of the present unpretending volume has sought to deal with the subject in a brief and interesting manner. If successful in, to some extent, drawing greater attention to our fast dying out customs and usages, the faults of a book, necessarily brief and fragmentary may be overlooked in the interest of the subject. The record of these customs is more than a matter of antiquarian curiosity, for it may help to throw light upon the life and the literature of Scotland in bygone days, and surely everything that enables us to understand our forefathers better is to be commended, and ought to be regarded as highly instructive.

CHAPTER II.

The Curfew—Curious Foot Ball Custom at Coldingham—Hand Ball—Rural Festival at Lochtie—Old Scottish Funeral Customs—Burgess Customs at Selkirk—Customs at Forfar commemorative of Queen Margaret—Charitable Feast at Kirkmichael—Singular Custom at South Queensferry—The Burry Man.

THE CURFEW.

OF our numerous ancient customs now rapidly falling into disuse with the March of the Centuries, none is more regretted by us than the cessation of the tolling of the Curfew. Musical Curfew! cradled amid the din of the Norman camp—dying out in our more peaceful Victorian era; in charming unison with the sweet calm of a summer's evenings are thy soft notes floating on the breeze. And yet of what a memorable and stormy epoch in our history do they not remind us? They tell of the time when our land was invaded by an invincible host who changed for us " our manners, our laws, our language, and our Kings "—of the days when the curfew of less troublous times was the *Couvre-Feu* of a Conqueror.

OLD FOOT AND HAND BALL GAMES.

On a particular day of the year set apart for the purpose, it was formerly the custom for the husbands and bachelors belonging to Coldingham to arrange themselves in opposing factions on the moor, and engage in a severe contest at the game of football; the former playing eastwards, and the latter towards the west. The sea shore formed a boundary for the married men; that of the un-married men was more difficult to get at, being a hole in the earth about a mile and a half west from the town. Latterly, the bachelors aimed at the barn-door of a farm steading which had been erected on the same site of ground. Under these favouring circumstances it is almost needless to say that the Benedicts were invariably victorious. Old and young turned out to view this favourite and exciting pastime, and the entire day was generally devoted to some kind of rural merry-making.

Foot and hand ball have long been favourite games with the people of Scotland. In olden times nearly every district had its annual *ba-playin*. The more expert at the pastime in one parish used to challenge those of another, and a sharp engagement was the result. The following were the rules observed on those occasions: It was not allowable to touch the ball with the hand after it had been cast upon the ground. An opponent might be tripped when near the ball, and more especially when about to hit it with his foot, but a competitor could not be laid hold of, or otherwise interfered with when at a distance from the ball, the party who out of three rounds hailed the ball twice was proclaimed victor. English forays were frequently conducted under the guise of football and handball matches. In the year 1600, Sir John Carmichael, Warden of the Middle Marches, was killed by a party of Armstrongs on their return from a game at football. Handball was more popular in the Southern districts, the most celebrated match of this last mentioned game which took place in modern times was played at Carterhaugh in the year 1815, the promoter of the match being the Earl of Home.

SPORTS IN FIFESHIRE.

On the summit of Benarty, which rises above Loch Orr, in the parish of Lochtie, in Fifeshire, there were formerly held games in which the Fifeshire herdsmen and those of the neighbouring counties were the performers. These came to the place of meeting accompanied by their wives, daughters, and sweethearts; and there being no lack of provisions, the fête was kept up for a few days, the revellers bivouacking during the night. Their chief games were the golf, the football, and the *Wads* (a pledge or hostage), what with howling, singing, and drinking, after the manner of the modern Irish, they contrived to spend a very happy time.

This rural custom is now abandoned, the number of herdsmen being much diminished, and the position not being of such convenience owing to the increased number of fences.

OLD FUNERAL CUSTOMS AT AVONDALE.

Much time was lost and no small expense incurred by the way in which funerals were conducted in the parish of Avondale and elsewhere, receiving their "service" in the barn or place of meeting. Though "warned" to attend at twelve o'clock, the guests seldom made their appearance till much later, and did not leave the place with the body before two o'clock. In general, three services were given; two glasses of wine and one of whisky or rum. Formerly, vast numbers of the friends and neighbours assembled to see the "chesting" or body put into the coffin. After which they generally drank tea, perhaps in the same room with the coffin.

In former times the ceremonies attendant on funerals were of a most singular nature. These varied according to the district. At the ancient Lyke-wake much unseemly mirth and revelling were formerly indulged in. In some of the more distant parishes the proceedings ended in a festival at the chesting of the corpse. Not unfrequently dancing as well as music followed part of these entertainments at Highland funerals, and when such a pastime was indulged in, to the relatives of the deceased was assigned the honour of opening the ball. While engaged in the duty of watching the dead prior to the funeral, the more sedate Lowlander generally confined himself to a silent process of drinking. The convivialities attendant on the death of a Highland chieftain in some instances proved nearly ruinous to his descendants. A succession of " Services " such as these in vogue in Avondale and Carluke, were common amongst the poorer classes in later times, and until very recently it was customary for crowds of beggars to come to the house from which a funeral had just departed, and receive the pence put aside for that benevolent purpose.

BURGESS CUSTOM AT SELKIRK.

A great trade in shoemaking was once carried on by the inhabitants of Selkirk, of which the only existing memorials are the old familiar song of the " Souters of Selkirk,"—

"Up wi' the Souters o' Selkirk
And down wi' the Earl of Home ;
And up wi' a' the braws lads
That sew the single-soled shoon.

"Fye upon yellow an' yellow,
Fye upon yellow an' green ; *
But up wi' the true blue an' scarlet,
An' up wi' the single-soled sheen.

"Up wi' the Souters o' Selkirk,
For they are baith trusty an' leal ;
An' down wi' the men o' the Merse,
An' the Earl may gang to the deil."

and the singular customs observed at the conferring the freedom of the burgh. Four or five bristles, such as are used by shoemakers, are attached to the seal of the burgess ticket. These the new made burgess must dip in his wine and pass through his mouth in token of respect for the Souters of Selkirk. The only instance of any remission of this disagreeable ritual was in favour of Prince Leopold (of course not the late Prince of that name), who was made a burgess in 1819. It is said, there is every reason to believe that the words of the old song allude to the battle of Flodden, and the different

---

* The liveries of the House of Home.

behaviour of the Souters, who distinguished themselves by their valour at Flodden, and of whom few survived to return from the fatal field, and the behaviour of Lord Home upon that occasion. At election times, when the Souters begin to get merry, they always call for music, and for that song in particular. A standard, the appearance of which bespeaks its antiquity, is still carried annually on the day of riding the Marches by the corporation of weavers, by a member of which it was taken from the English on the field of Flodden.

THE GRACE CUP.

It would appear from ancient historical records that the old county town of Forfar owed much to the munificence of Margaret Atheling, Queen of Malcolm Canmore, whose piety and good works won for her the proud designation of St. Margaret of Scotland. And tradition, it is said, celebrates her attention to the instruction of the young women of Forfar. In order to evince their gratitude to their beloved Queen for the many benefits conferred upon the town, the inhabitants made a holiday of the 19th of June, in memory of her, and instituted an annual ball in her honour. St. Margaret did much to overcome the natural roughness of the Scottish nobles, as well as their carelessness in the matter of religious observances; and it was the law of her table that none should drink after dinner who did not wait the giving of thanks. Hence the origin of the phrase known throughout Scotland of the *Grace Cup*.

OLD CUSTOM AT KIRKMICHAEL.

"Bear ye one another's burdens" seems to have been one of the Bible precepts that were formerly reduced to practice by the inhabitants of Kirkmichael. It is recorded of the old parishioners that when any of the poorer classes were reduced by sickness, losses or any other kind of misfortune, a friend was sent to as many of their neighbours as they thought requisite, to invite them to what they called a "drinking." This drinking consisted of a little beer, with a piece of bread and cheese, and sometimes a small glass of brandy or whisky, previously provided by the needy persons or their friends. The guests assembled at the time appointed, and after the people of the house had received from each a shilling, and perhaps more, the company amused themselves for about a couple of hours with music and dancing, and then went home. Such as could not attend themselves usually sent their charitable contributions by any neighbour who chose to go. These meetings sometimes produced from five to seven pounds for the distressed person or family.

THE BURRY MAN.

A singular custom observed even at the present day amongst the youth of Queensferry has been supposed to commemorate there the passage of Malcolm Canmore and Queen Margaret to and from Edinburgh to Dunfermline, and to indicate the origin of the place. The observance referred to is the annual procession of the " Burry Man," got up on the day preceding the annual fair, amongst the boys of Queensferry, and which was thus described in the Journals of the day— The annual saturnalia of the ancient port of passage over the Firth of St. Margaret the Queen, came off on Friday 9th August, having been preceded on Thursday 8th, according to ancient customs, by the singular perambulation of the Burry Man, i.e., a man or lad clad loosely in flannels stuck over with the well-known adhesive bur of the *Arctimus Bardana* (the bur thistle) of Burns, though in reality not a thistle but a burdock as botanists can aver.

The burrs are found in considerable profusion at Blackness Point in the immediate vicinity of Hopeton House. A few plants also grow in the neighbourhood of New Halls Point, and beyond the rocks of the opposite shore of North Queensferry where we have found it on the Links near Inverkeithing; and from all these and even more remote places are they gathered if necessary, for this occasion. So essential are they deemed to the maintenance of the curious ceremony, the origin and object of which are lost in antiquity, and long ago foiled the antiquarian research of Sir Walter Scott. Tradition at present connects the custom with the erection of Queensferry into a royal burgh, which did not take place till the time of Charles I., and even points to the previous constitution as a burgh of regality, alleged to have been originated under Malcolm Caen-Mohr, in which case the representation of the burgh by the Burry Man would amount to a whimsical, practical pun. The custom in question can be traced back to the period of the last battle of Falkirk; for an old woman of 80, whose dead mother was aged 13 at the date of the battle (1746) stated that the observance has been unaltered from then till now.

On the day preceding the fair, the Burry Man, who requires to be either a stout man or robust lad, is encased in flannels, face, arms, and legs all being covered so as to resemble as closely as possible a man in chain armour from the close adhesion of the burrs. The hands as well as the tops of two staves grasped with extended arms, are beautifully adorned with flowers. The victim thus accoutred is led from door to door by two attendants who likewise assist in upholding his arms by grasping the staves. At every door in succession a shout is raised and the inhabitants come forth bestowing their kindly greetings and donations of money on the Burry Man, who in this way generally collects, we believe, considerable sums which are equally divided and spent at the fair by the youths associated in the exploit.

Sometimes there are two persons thus selected and led in procession from door to door, the one being styled the King and the other the Queen, in allusion to the passage of the royal couple through the burgh. An ingenious author adapting his description to the royal visit of 1822, has even gone the length of adducing the particulars of the burgh arms as confirmatory of the origin of the observance under Malcolm III. The town's arms consist, 1st, of a ship; 2nd, of a fine figure of a youthful female in the act of landing; 3rd, a cross to represent Margaret's attachment to the Christian faith, and four or five sea fowls said to have appeared near the spot where the Queen landed. It is, or used to be, a popular belief that the giving up of this quaint custom would be productive of misfortune to the town.

CHAPTER III.

Women playing at foot ball—Singular wedding custom in Ayrshire and the Border—The ancient game of golf—Unpleasant Burgess custom at Edinburgh—The Robin Hood games—The Poor Folks in Edinburgh—The Siller Square—Customs in connection with the Blue Blanket banner—The old custom of Handfasting.

WOMEN PLAYING AT FOOTBALL.

IN the ancient burgh of Musselburgh, on Shrove Tuesday, there used to be a standing match at football between the married and unmarried fishwomen, in which the former were always victorious. No doubt the knowledge that their victory would reflect honour on their "gudemen and bairns" would nerve the arm and impart vigour to the stroke of the Musselburgh matrons on the occasion of these animated contests.

SINGULAR WEDDING CUSTOMS.

When a young man went to pay his addresses to his sweetheart, instead of going to her father and declaring his passion, he adjourned to a public-house, and, having made a confidante of his landlady, the object of his attachment was at once sent for. The fair maiden thus honoured seldom refused to come; and the marriage was arranged over constant supplies of ale, whisky, and brandy! The common form of betrothal on such occasions was as follows: the parties linked the thumbs of their right hands, which they pressed together, and vowed fidelity.

> " My sweetest May, let love incline ye,
> Accept a heart which he designs ye;
> And as you cannot, love, regret it,
> Syne for its faithfulness receive it.
> 'Tis proof as shot to birth or money,
> But yields to what is sweet and bonny;

> Receive it, then, wi' a kiss and a smiley,
> There's my thumb, it will ne'er beguile ye."

On the second day after their wedding, a creeling, as it is called, took place. That is, the newly-wedded pair and their friends assembled in a field agreed upon, and into a small basket or creel some stones were placed. This burden the young men of the party carried alternately, allowing themselves to be caught and kissed by the maidens who accompanied them. After a great deal of innocent mirth and pleasantry, the creel fell at length to the young husband's share, who was generally obliged to carry it for a considerable length of time, none of the young women appearing to take compassion on him. At last his fair partner flew to the rescue, and kindly relieved him of his burden. . The creel went round again, more fun ensued, then the entire company dined together and talked over the events of the day. This custom, which was generally practised in Border villages and in some parts of Ayrshire and elsewhere, was believed to shadow forth the cares a man incurred by marrying, but of which it was in the power of a good wife to relieve him.

Marriage customs, in common with those attendant on funerals, were formerly of an extravagant and peculiar character. When country couples were about to marry, all manner of contributions were showered upon them by their neighbours and friends. In olden times, it was customary for those who intended being present at the marriage to bestow a Penny Scots on the youthful pair; hence originated the term of Penny, or Paying Wedding. The festivities indulged in on those occasions frequently extended over several days, and such scenes of riot ensued in consequence of the heavy drinking that these Penny Weddings were at length condemned by the General Assembly.

THE ROYAL SCOTTISH GAME.

Golf is an amusement said to be peculiar to Scotland. In Edinburgh, it has been a favourite pastime from time immemorial. By a statute of King James II., it was prohibited that it might not interfere with the "weapon shawings." These were assemblies of the populace in military array and properly armed, which were organised by the Sheriff of every county at least twice in the year. Golf is commonly played on rugged ground covered with short grass upon the seashore, called in Scotland *Links*. This popular pastime is usually played by parties of one or more on each side. Each person provides himself with balls and a set of clubs. The ball is extremely hard, and about the size of a tennis ball. The club with which the ball is usually struck is slender and elastic, crooked at the end, which is faced with horn, and headed with lead to render it heavy. A set of clubs consists of five in number—a play club, a scraper, a spoon, an iron-headed club, and a short club called a *putter*. The second, third, and fourth of these are adopted for removing the ball from the various inconvenient positions into which it may come in the course of the game. The putter is used when a short stroke is intended. The game is played thus:—Small holes are made in the ground at the distance of about a quarter of a mile from each other, and in such a direction as to encompass the whole field. The game is won by the party who lodges his balls in the different holes in succession with the fewest strokes. The art of the game consists, first, at the outset, in striking the ball to a great distance and in a proper direction so that it may rest upon smooth ground; secondly, and this is of the greatest importance, when near the hole so to proportionate the force and direction of the stroke, or *putting*, as it is called, that the ball may with a few strokes be driven into the hole. Golf is a Scottish game of great antiquity. Although prohibited by James II., it was a popular pastime in the reign of James VI., who practised it himself while at Dunfermline, and introduced it afterwards at Blackheath, in Kent. During his residence in Scotland, in 1641, Charles I. played golf on the links at Leith. His royal brother, James VII., was also devoted to this national sport. The headquarters of golf is at St. Andrews; and the rules authorised by its club are adopted by all the other golfing societies throughout the country.

BURGESS CUSTOM AT EDINBURGH.

In the "good old times" an annual procession took place at Edinburgh on the King's birthday, when every new burgess who presented himself was initiated by the disagreeable process of a bumping against a stone.

THE ROBIN HOOD GAMES.

The Robin Hood Games were enacted with great vivacity at various places, but particularly at Edinburgh; and in connection with them were the sports of the *Abbot of Disobedience*, or *Unreason*, a strange, half serious burlesque on some of the ecclesiastical arrangements then prevalent, and also a representation called the *Queen of May*. A noted historical work * thus describes what took place at these whimsical merrymakings—"At the approach of May, the people assembled and chose some respectable individuals of their number—very grave and reverend citizens perhaps—to act the parts of Robin Hood and Little John, of the Lord of Disobedience or the Abbot of Unreason, and make sports and jocosities of them. If the chosen actors felt it inconsistent with their tastes, gravity, or engagements, to don a fantastic dress, caper and dance, and incite their neighbours to do the like, they would only be excused on paying a fine. On the appointed day, always a Sunday or holiday, the people assembled in their best attire and in military

---

* *The Domestic Annals of Scotland.*

array, and marched in blythe procession to some neighbouring field, where the fitting preparations had been made for their amusement. Robin Hood and Little John robbed bishops, fought with pinners, and contended in archery among themselves as they had done in reality two centuries before. The Abbot of Unreason kicked up his heels and played antics like a modern pantaloon. Maid Marian also appeared upon the scene in flower-spirit kirtle, and with bow and arrows in hand, and doubtless slew *hearts* as she had formerly done *harts*. Mingling with the mad scene were the Morris-dancers, with their fantastic dresses and gingling bells. And so it continued till the Reformation, when a sudden stop was put to the whole affair by severe penalties imposed by Act of Parliament."*

PRIVILEGED BEGGARS.

Chambers, in his "Traditions of Edinburgh," gives us the following in connection with a curious local custom—" In that part of the High Street named the Luckenbooths, and directly opposite to the ancient prison

---

* *The Book of Days.*

house, stood two lands of old houses. Getting old and crazy the western tenement was entirely demolished, but the eastern portion was only refreshed with a new front of stonework. The remaining building was formerly the lodging of Adam Bothwell, Commendator of Holyrood House, who is remarkable for his having performed the marriage ceremony of Queen Mary and the hated Bothwell. At the back of this house there is a projection, on the top of which is a bartizan or level roof, and there is a tradition that Oliver Cromwell lived in this lodging and used to come and sit here to view his navy on the Forth. This large pile of building was called 'Poor Folks Purses' from this singular circumstance. It was formerly the custom for the privileged beggars known as 'Blue Gowns' to assemble in the Palace yard, when a small donation from the King was conferred on each of them. After receiving this dole they marched in procession up the High Street, till they came to this spot, when the magistrates gave each a *leathern purse*, and a small sum of money. The ceremony concluded by their proceeding to the High Church to hear a sermon from one of the King's chaplains.

PROCURING SILVER SPOONS.

Parliament Close, Edinburgh, being the well known resort of the Goldsmiths, it was here that country couples came for the purchase of their silver spoons on entering upon holy matrimony. In olden times it was quite customary in the country for intending bridegrooms to take a journey a few weeks previous to their marriage to the Parliament Close to purchase their *siller spoons*. This important transaction occasioned two journeys: one to select the spoons and furnish the initials to be marked upon them; the other to receive and pay for them.

CUSTOMS IN CONNECTION WITH THE BLUE BANNER.

This was the ancient banner of the trades of Edinburgh. On its appearance, not only the artificers of Edinburgh were obliged to repair to it, but all the artificers or craftsmen within Scotland were bound to follow and fight under the Convener who took charge of it. According to an old tradition, this standard was employed in the Holy Wars by a body of crusading citizens of Edinburgh, and was the first that was planted on the walls of Jerusalem, when that city was stormed by the Christian army under the famous Godfrey de Bouillon. It is told in connection with this standard, that James III., having been kept a prisoner for nine months in the Castle of Edinburgh, by his rebellious nobles, was freed by the citizens of Edinburgh, who raised the Blue Blanket, assaulted the Castle and took it by surprise. Out of gratitude for their seasonable loyalty, James, besides certain privileges, presented them with *another* banner—a blue silken pennon, with powers to display the same in defence of their King, country, and their own rights, when these were assailed. The original and more celebrated banner is, we are glad to be able to state, also still in existence, and was exhibited at the opening of St. Giles' Church.

THE CUSTOM OF HAND-FASTING.

In Catholic times the practice known as Hand-fasting was pretty general in Scotland. It was supposed to have originated from the want of Clergy, but from habit was continued by the people after the Reformation had supplied them with ministers. According to tradition, a spot at the junction of waters known as the Black and White Esk, was remarkable in former times for an annual fair which had been held there from time immemorial, but which exists no longer. At that fair it was customary for the unmarried of both sexes to choose a companion, according to their fancy, with whom to live till that time next year. This was called *handfasting*, or *hand-in-fist*. If the parties remained pleased with each other at the expiry of the term of probation, they remained together for life; if not, they separated, and were free to provide themselves with another partner. From the various monasteries priests were sent into the surrounding districts to look after all hand-fasted persons, and to bestow the nuptial benediction on those who were willing to receive it. Thus, when Eskdale belonged to the Abbey of Melrose, a priest on whom was bestowed the name, " Book-i-the-bosom," either because he carried a prayer book in his bosom, or perhaps a register of the marriage, came from time to time to confirm the irregular union contracted at this fair.

This singular custom was known to have been sometimes taken advantage of by persons of rank. Lindsay, in his account of the reign of James II., says, "that James, Sixth Earl of

Murray, had a son by Isabel Innes, daughter of the Laird of Innes, Alexander Dunbar, a man of singular wit and courage. This Isabel was but hand-fasted to him, and deceased before the marriage." If either of the parties insisted on a separation, and a child was born during the year of trial, it was to be taken care of by the father only, and to be ranked among his lawful children next after his heirs. The offspring was not treated as illegitimate, because the custom was justified being such, and instituted with a view of making way for a peaceful and happy marriage. Such was also the power of custom, that the apprenticeship for matrimony brought no reproach on the separated lady; and, if her character was good, she was entitled to an equal match as though nothing had happened. It is said that a desperate feud ensued between the clans of Macdonald of Sleat, and Macleod of Dunvegan, owing to the former chief having availed himself of this licence to send back the sister or daughter of the latter. Macleod, resenting the indignity, observed, "that since there was no wedding bonfire there should be one to solemnize the divorce." Accordingly, he burned and laid waste the territories of the Macdonalds, who retaliated, and a dreadful feud with all its horrors took place in consequence.

Hand-fasting was deemed a social irregularity by the Reformers, and they strove by every means to repress it. In 1562, the Kirk-Session of Aberdeen decreed that all hand-fasted persons should be married. With the exception of the Highland districts, the time-honoured practice of living together for "a year and a day" ceased to exist shortly after the Reformation.

CHAPTER IV.

The Herds' Festival at Midlothian—Old customs in connection with Archery—The Hangman's right at Dumfries—The Cure for Scolds at Langholm—Customs regarding Holy wells—Curious customs at Rutherglen—The feast of Sour Cakes—Riding the Marches—Foot-Race at Biggar—Riding the Stang.

THE HERDS' FESTIVAL AT MIDLOTHIAN.

ABOUT a century ago, the 1st of August was celebrated as follows by the herds of Midlothian :—Early in summer the herds associated themselves in bands—each band proceeded to erect a tower in a central locality to serve as a place of meeting on Lammas. The tower was built of sods; and was generally four feet in diameter at the base, and tapered towards the summit, which rose about eight feet from the ground. There was a hole in the centre for the insertion of a flag staff. The building of the tower commenced a month before Lammas. For the space of this month one of the builders kept watch in order to prevent its being attacked by any of the rival communities. This warder was provided with a horn which he sounded in case of an assault. On the approach of Lammas each party appointed a captain. He was entrusted with the duty of bearing the standard, (a towel borrowed from some farmer's wife) decorated with ribbons and attached to a pole. On the morning of the festival he displayed this flag on the summit of the tower. The assembled herdsmen waited under his leadership, to resist an assault of the enemy. Scouts were dispatched at intervals to ascertain whether any foe was near. When menaced by danger horns were blown, and the little army marched forth to meet the advancing enemy. At some engagements a hundred combatants would appear on each side. After a short struggle the stronger party yielded to the weaker; but there were instances in which such mimic warfare terminated in bloodshed. If no enemy appeared before the hour of noon, the garrison removed their standards and marched to the nearest village, where they concluded the day's amusements with foot-races and other diversions.

OLD ARCHERY CUSTOMS.

The ancient and once royal sport of archery was much encouraged in Scotland by James I. In his reign men were required to "busk themselves archers" from the early age of twelve years. James V. presented silver arrows to the royal burghs, to which the winners in the annual competitions might affix silver medals as memorials of their skill. The Edinburgh Company of Archers is privileged to rank as the Queen's Scottish Body-guard. There were two kinds of archery, point blank archery, i.e., shooting at "butts," and popinjay archery, such as that occasionally practised by the members of the Kilwinning Archery Club, and described as follows :—The ancient custom of shooting at the popinjay existed at Kilwinning as far back as the year 1488. The popinjay is a bird known in heraldry. It was cut out of wood, fixed at the end of a pole, and placed at a distance of a hundred and twenty feet on the steeple of the Abbey. The archer who brought down the mark was honoured with the title of Captain of the Popinjay, and received a parti-coloured sash. He was master of the ceremonies for the ensuing year. He sent cards of invitation to the ladies, gave them a splendid ball, and transmitted his honours by a medal with suitable devices affixed to a silver arrow.

SINGULAR CUSTOM IN CONNECTION WITH THE OFFICE OF HANGMAN AT DUMFRIES.

The following singular custom formerly existed in Dumfries:—The county hangman went through the market every market day furnished with a brass ladle or large spoon, pushed it into the mouth of every sack of meal, corn, etc., and carried it off full. The small quantity of meal so abstracted was termed a "lock," and, when spoken of, the hangman was frequently alluded to as the "lockman." When the farmers refused any longer to comply with this custom, the matter was brought before the law courts, and the hangman was found to have a right to the perquisite of office. In consequence of this decision, many of the farmers refused for a long time to send their meal and corn to this market.

THE CURE FOR SCOLDS AT LANGHOLM.

Langholm was long ago famous for an iron instrument called the "Branks," which fitted upon the head of a shrewish female, and projecting a sharp spike into her mouth, effectually silenced the organ of speech. It was formerly customary for husbands who were afflicted with scolding wives, to subject their heads to this instrument, and lead them through the town, exposed to the laughter and reproaches of the people. Tradition affirms that the discipline never failed to effect a complete reformation. "The Branks," so Dr. Platt observes, "was much to be preferred to the ducking stool, which not only endangered the health of the patient, but gave the tongue liberty between each dip."

CUSTOMS REGARDING HOLY WELLS.

The remedial qualities of certain wells

were, it would appear, well known to the ancients. The Roman and Greek physicians were familiar with their efficacy. The Orientals again attributed the cures effected by their means to supernatural agency. Our own heathen forefathers believed that wells were originally constructed by demons or devils for the destruction of mankind, but that the Saints had interfered to prevent their malignant design, and by their prayers had succeeded in transforming what was formerly intended to prove a curse into an inestimable blessing. In many instances, however, the ancient worship of Neith, the Goddess of Waters, was accountable for the reverence in which certain reputed wells were formerly held by the populace; and after the Reformation a clerical raid was instituted against the so-styled " heathenish well worship."

There were formerly three wells in the parish of Culsalmond, St. Mary's Well on the farm of Calpie, St. Michael's at Gateside, and another at the foot of the Culsalmond bank, a little to the west of the Lady's Causeway. On the first Sunday of May, multitudes resorted to them from distant parts, in the full belief that by washing in the stream and leaving presents to the saints, as their heathen ancestors did to the spirits presiding over the well, they would be cured of their diseases. Pieces of money were always left in the water corresponding to the circumstances of the afflicted persons. Some time ago while digging a drain at the foot of the bank, the workman stuck his pick into the back of the well which had been there; a large quantity of water sprung up into the air, in which he observed a shining substance. This proved on inspection to be a gold piece of James I. of Scotland as perfect as when it came from the mint.

SINGULAR CUSTOM AT RUTHERGLEN.

The ancient town of Rutherglen was long famous throughout the country, for the singular custom of baking what was called "sour cakes" about eight or ten days before St. Luke's fair—for they were baked at no other time in the year. A certain quantity of meal was made into dough with warm water, and laid up in a vessel to ferment. Being brought to a proper degree of fermentation and consistency, it was rolled up into balls proportionable to the intended size of the cakes. With the dough there was commonly mixed a small quantity of sugar and a little anise seed or cinnamon. The baking was executed by women only, and they seldom began their work till after sunset, and a night or two before the fair. A large space of the house chosen for the purpose, was marked out by a line drawn upon it. The area within it was considered consecrated ground, and was not to be touched by any of the bystanders with impunity. Every trespasser paid a small fine, which was always laid out in liquor for the use of the company.

This hallowed spot was occupied by six or eight women, all of whom, except the toaster, seated themselves on the ground in a circular form having their feet turned towards the fire. Each of them was provided with a bakeboard, about two feet square, which they held on their knees. The woman who toasted the cakes, which she did on an iron plate suspended over the fire, was called the *queen* or *bride*, and the others were styled her *maidens*. These were distinguished from one another by names given them for the occasion. She who sat next the fire towards the east was called *todler*. Her companion on the left hand was called the *hodler*.* And the rest had arbitrary names given them by the bride, as Mrs. Baker, *best* and *worst* maids, etc.

The operation was begun by the todler, who took a ball, formed it into a small cake, and then cast it on the bakeboard of the hodler, who beat it out a little thinner. This being done, she in her turn threw it on the board of her neighbour, and thus it went round from east to west, *in the direction of the sun's course*, until it came to the toaster, by which time it was as thin as a piece of paper. Sometimes the cake was so thin as to be carried by the air up the chimney?

As the baking was wholly performed by the hand a great deal of noise was the consequence. The beats, however, were not irregular nor destitute of an agreeable harmony, especially when they were accompanied with vocal music, which was frequently the case. Great dexterity was necessary not only to beat out the cakes with no other implements than the hand so that no part of the cake

---

* These names were descriptive of the manner in which the women so called performed their part of the work. To *todle* is to walk slowly like a child. To *hodle* is to move about more quickly.

should be thicker than another, but especially to cast them on each other's boards without ruffling or breaking them.

The toaster required considerable skill, for which reason the most experienced person in the company was chosen for that part of the work. One cake was sent round in quick succession to another, so that none of the company were suffered to remain idle. The scene was one of activity, mirth, and diversion.

As there is no account even handed down by tradition respecting the origin of this custom it must be very ancient. The bread thus baked was doubtless never meant for human use. It is difficult to conceive how mankind, especially in a rude age, would strictly observe so many ceremonies, and take such great pains in making a cake which, when folded together, made but a small mouthful. Besides it was always given away in presents to strangers who frequented the fair.

The custom seems originally to have been derived from paganism, and to contain not a few of the sacred rites peculiar to that impure belief: such as the leavened dough, and the mixing it with sugar and spices; the consecrated ground, etc. But the particular deity for whose use these cakes were first made, is not easy to determine. Probably it was no other than the one known in scripture (Jer. v. ii. 18.) by the name of the *Queen of Heaven*, and to whom cakes were likewise kneaded by women. This custom is now obsolete.

Besides baking *sour cakes* it was formerly the practice to prepare *salt roasts* for St. Luke's fair. Till of late years almost every house in Rutherglen was furnished with dozens of them. They were the chief articles of provisions asked for by strangers who frequented the fair.

RIDING THE MARCHES AT RUTHERGLEN.

The Riding of the Marches is an ancient "burghal celebration," and was very requisite when written documents were in constant danger of being destroyed. In former times lands had been bestowed by the sovereign on most of the towns where the ceremony was and is still observed. The boundaries of such possessions came to be determined by processions, etc.; and although in the course of time these lands passed into other hands, the old custom of "marking the boundaries" in accordance with the ancient fashion was still retained. At Rutherglen the ceremony was performed in the following manner:—The Magistrates with a considerable number of the Council and inhabitants assembled at the Cross, from which they proceeded in martial order with drums beating; and in that manner went round the boundaries of the Royalty to see if any encroachments had been made upon them. These boundaries were distinguished by march-stones set up at some little distance from each other. In some places there were two rows about seven feet apart. The stones were shaped at the top like a man's head, but the lower part was square. This peculiar figure was originally intended to represent the god *Terminus*, of whom there were formerly so many rude representations.

It was a custom from time immemorial for the riders of the marches to dress their hats and drums with broom, and to combat with one another at the newly erected stone, out of respect perhaps to the deity whose image they had set up, or that they might the better remember the precise boundaries at that place. This part of the ceremony was afterwards postponed till the survey was over and the company had returned to the Cross, when, having previously provided themselves with broom, they had a mock engagement, and fought seemingly with great fury till their weapons failed them, when they parted in good fellowship.

OLD CUSTOMS AT BIGGAR.

In the parish of Biggar there were formerly held three fairs,—Candlemas fair, Midsummer fair, and the old Biggar fair, held on the last Thursday of October O.S. On the evening previous to the Midsummer fair, it was formerly the custom for the Baron Bailie to advertise that a foot race would be run along the streets, and that a pair of gloves would be the prize. It was also an ancient custom, and one which frequently caused much rioting and confusion, to throw out a football.

The young men immediately divided themselves into two parties. The ball, which was made of leather stuffed with wool, was thrown up at the Cross in the centre of the town. The party who could kick the ball, in spite of their antagonists, to the other end of the village, were the victors. No prize was awarded in this contest.

In connection with Biggar, Forsyth in his

"Beauties of Scotland," relates that "here as well as in other places in Scotland a very singular practice is at times, though very rarely, revived. This is called "Riding the Stang." When any husband was known to beat his wife, and when this offence was long continued, while the wife's character was known to be spotless, the indignation of the neighbourhood becoming gradually greater, at length broke out in the following manner. All the women entered into a conspiracy to execute vengeance on the culprit. Having fixed on a particular day for the prosecution of their design, they suddenly assembled in a great crowd and seized the offending party, they taking care at the same time to provide a stout beam of wood upon which they set him astride, and bore him aloft, his legs tied beneath. He was then carried in derision through the village attended by the hootings, scoffings, and hisses of his numerous attendants, who pulled down his legs so as to render his position a very uneasy one. The grown up men in the meantime remained at a distance and avoided interfering in the matter. It was lucky for the culprit at the conclusion of the ceremony if a ducking was not added to the rest of the punishment. The origin of this custom is unknown.

CHAPTER V.

Old Marriage Customs in Perthshire—Superstitions regarding the cure of disease—Scottish customs regarding the observance of Hallow e'en—General description of this festival—Pulling the Green Kail—Eating the Apple—Burning Nuts—Sowing Hemp Seed—Winnowing Corn—Measuring the Bean Stack—Eating the Herring—Dipping the Shirt Sleeve—The Three Plates—Throwing the Clue—Illustrative Anecdote—Pricking the Egg—The Summons of Death.

MARRIAGE CUSTOMS.

IN the parish of Logierait, Perthshire, and its neighbourhood, a variety of superstitious customs formerly prevailed amongst the vulgar. Lucky and unlucky days were by many annually observed. That day of the week upon which the 14th of May happened to follow was esteemed unlucky throughout the remainder of the year. None got married or began any serious business upon it. None chose to marry in January or May; or to have their banns proclaimed in the end of one quarter of the year and to marry in the beginning of the next. Some things were to be done before the full moon, others after. In fevers the patient was expected to be worse on Sundays than on the other days of the week; did he, however, prove to be better on that day a relapse was dreaded.

Immediately before the celebration of the marriage ceremony, every knot about the bride and bridegroom's dress, garters, shoe-strings, petticoat-strings, etc., were carefully loosed. After leaving the church the whole company walked round it keeping the church walls carefully on their right hand. The bridegroom, however, first retired one way with some young men to tie the knots that were loosed about him; while the bride in the same manner withdrew to put her array in order.

BAPTISMAL CUSTOM.

When a child was baptised privately it was formerly the custom to put the child into a clean basket, having over it a cloth containing bread and cheese. The basket was then moved three times successively round the iron *crook* which hangs suspended from the roof, over the fire for the purpose of supporting the pot, in which water is boiled and food prepared. It is supposed that this custom was originally intended to counteract the malignant arts which witches and evil spirits were supposed to practise against new born children.

THE CURE OF DISEASE.

Recourse was often had to charms for the cure of diseases of horses and cows as well as those of the human race. In the case of various diseases in this parish a pilgrimage was performed to a place called Strathfillan, forty miles distant from Logierait. Here the patient bathed in a certain pool and performed some other rites in a chapel close at hand. It is chiefly in cases of madness that a pilgrimage to Strathfillan was considered salutary. The afflicted person was first bathed in the pool, then left bound all night in the chapel. If found loose in the morning he was expected to recover.

There was a disease called Claeach by the Highlanders, which, as it affected the chest and lungs, was evidently of a consumptive nature. It was also called the "Macdonald disease," because there were particular tribes of the Macdonalds who were believed to cure it with the charms of their touch and a certain form of words. No fee was given. The Highlanders' faith in the touch of a Macdonald was very great.

ALL HALLOW'S EVE OBSERVANCES.

One of the former four great Fire festivals in Britain, is supposed, as previously stated, to have taken place on the 1st of November, when all fires save those of the Druids were extinguished, and, from whose altars only, the holy fire must be purchased by the householders for a certain price. The festival is still known in Ireland, as Samhein, or La Samon, *i.e.*, the Feast of the Sun; while in Scotland, it has assumed the name of Hallowe'en.

> "The night is Hallowe'en, Janet,
> The morn is Hallowes day,
> And gin ye dare your true love win
> Ye hae nae time to stay.
>
> "The night it is good Hallowe'en,
> When fairy folk will ride,
> And they that wad their true love win
> At Miles Cross they must bide."

All Hallow's Eve, as observed in the Church of Rome, corresponds with the Feralia of the ancient Romans, when they sacrificed in honour of the dead; offered up prayers for them, and made oblations to them. In ancient times, this festival was celebrated on the twenty-first of February, but the Romish Church transferred it in her Calendar to the first of November. It was originally designed to give rest and peace to the souls of the departed. In some parts of Scotland, it is still customary for young people to kindle fires on the tops of hills and rising grounds, and fire of this description goes by the name of a Hallowe'en bleeze. Formerly it was customary to surround these bonfires with a circular trench symbolical of the sun. Sheriff Barclay tells us that about fifty years ago while travelling from Dunkeld to Aberfeldy on Hallowe'en, he counted thirty fires blazing on the hill tops, with the phantom figures of persons dancing round the flames.

In Perthshire the Hallowe'en bleeze is made in the following picturesque fashion. Heath, broom, and dressings of flax are tied upon a pole. The faggot is then kindled ; a youth takes it upon his shoulders and carries it about. When the faggot is burned out a second is tied to the pole and kindled in the same manner as the former one. Several of these blazing faggots are often carried through the villages at the same time. Should the night be dark they form a fine illumination.

Hallowe'en is believed by the superstitious in Scotland to be a night on which the invisible world has peculiar power. His Satanic Majesty is supposed to have great latitude allowed him on this anniversary, in common with that oft malignant class of beings known as witches; some of whom, it is said, may be seen cleaving the air on broomsticks, in a manner wondrous to behold. Others again less aerially disposed jog comfortably along over by-road and heath, seated on the back of such sleek tabby cats as have kindly allowed themselves to be transformed—*pro tem.*—into coal-black steeds for the accommodation of these capricious old ladies.

The green-robed fays are also said to hold special festive meetings at their favourite haunts :—

> " Tis Hallowmasses e'en
> And round the holy green
> The fairy elves are seen
> Tripping light."

The ignorant believe that there is no such

night in all the year for obtaining an insight into futurity. The following are the customs pertaining to this eve of mystic ceremonies:—The youths and maidens, who engage in the ceremony of Pulling the Green Kail go hand in hand, with shut eyes, into a bachelor's or spinster's garden, and pull up the first "kail stalks" which come in their way. Should the stalks thus secured prove to be of stately growth, straight in stem, and with a goodly supply of earth at their roots, the future husbands (or wives) will be young, good-looking, and rich in proportion. But if the stalks be stunted, crooked, and hence little or no earth at their roots, the future spouses will be found lacking in good looks and fortune. According as the heart or stem proves sweet or sour to the taste so will be the temper of the future partner. The stalks thus tasted are afterwards placed above the doors of the respective houses, and the christian names of those persons who first pass underneath will correspond with those of the future husbands or wives.

There is also the custom of Eating the Apple at the Glass. Provide yourself with an apple, and, as the clock strikes twelve, go alone into a room where there is a looking-glass. Cut the apple into small pieces; throw one of them over your left shoulder, and advancing to the mirror without looking back, proceed to eat the remainder, combing your hair carefully the while before the glass. While thus engaged, it is said, that the face of the person you are to marry will be seen peeping over your left shoulder. This Hallowe'en game is supposed to be a relic of that form of divinations with mirrors which was condemned as sorcery by the former Popes.

Likewise that of Burning Nuts. Take two nuts and place them in the fire, bestowing on one of them your own name; on the other that of the object of your affections. Should they burn quietly away side by side, then the issue of your love affair will be prosperous; but if one starts away from the other, the result will be unfavourable.

And for the Sowing Hemp Seed, steal forth alone towards midnight and sow a handful of hemp seed, repeating the following rhyme:—

"Hemp seed, I sow thee, hemp seed I sow thee;
And he that is my true love come behind and harrow me."

Then look over your left shoulder and you will see the person thus adjured in the act of harrowing.

The ceremony of Winnowing Corn must also be gone through in solitude. Go to the barn and open both doors, taking them off the hinges if possible, lest the being you expect to appear, may close them and do you some injury. Then take the instrument used in winnowing corn, and go through all the attitudes of letting it down against the wind. Repeat the operation three times, and the figure of your future partner will appear passing in at one door and out at the other. Should those engaging in this ceremony be fated to die young it is believed that a coffin, followed by mourners, will enter and pursue the too adventurous youth or maiden, who thus wishes to pry into the hidden things of the future, round the barn.

Another is Measuring the Bean Stack. Go three times round a bean stack with outstretched arms, as if measuring it, and the third time you will clasp in your arms the shade of your future partner.

As also Eating the Herring. Just before retiring to rest eat a raw or roasted salt herring; and in your dreams your husband (or wife) that is to be, will come and offer you a drink of water to quench your thirst.

For Dipping the Shirt Sleeve. Go alone, or in company with others, to a stream where "three lairds' lands meet," and dip in the left sleeve of a shirt; after this is done not one word must be spoken, otherwise the spell is broken. Then put your sleeve to dry before your bed-room fire. Go to bed, but be careful to remain awake, and you will see the form of your future help-mate enter and turn the sleeve in order that the other side may get dried.

Likewise the Three Plates. Place three plates in a row on a table. In one of these put clean water, in another foul, and leave the third empty. Blindfold the person wishing to try his or her fortune, and lead them up to the table. The left hand must be put forward. Should it come in contact with the clean water, then the future spouse will be young, handsome, and a bachelor or maid. The foul signifies a widower or a widow; and the empty dish, single blessedness. This ceremony is repeated three times, and the plates must be differently arranged after each attempt.

Also Throwing the Clue. Steal forth alone and at night, to the nearest lime-kiln, and throw in a clue of blue yarn, winding it off on to a fresh clue. As you come near the end some one will grasp hold of the thread lying in the kiln. You then ask, "Who holds?" when the name of your future partner will be uttered from beneath.

The following truthful anecdote will serve to illustrate the implicit belief our simple—need we add, credulous—Scottish maidens used to place in the mystic rite. In the parish in which the editor of this volume at one time resided, there lived a very pretty girl called Mary Shirley. Mary had two lovers, respectively named Robert Lawrie and William Fleming. The former of these youths was the favoured one. In his despair, for he was devotedly attached to the fair maiden, Fleming repaired to her most intimate friend and implored her by every means in her power to further his suit. Feeling deeply for the poor youth, and esteeming him, as indeed he was, the most worthy of the lovers, this girl informed him, in the strictest confidence, that

Mary Shirley intended on the coming Hallowe'en to throw the blue clue into the kiln nearest her father's house. Fleming obeyed the hint thus kindly given him. On the night in question, he hid himself in the kiln, and seized hold of the clue which his agitated Mary threw in. In answer to her faltering "Who holds?" he gave his own name. Hastily dropping the thread, the terrified girl fled homewards. Ere many days had elapsed, Fleming proposed to, and was accepted by the pretty Mary, to the no small surprise and anger of his rival.

When congratulated on the wisdom of her choice the blushing maiden replied, "it was na me wha made the choice. I mysell was a' for Robert, but fate had it I was tae get the ither, and wha can gang again fate?" The marriage thus strangely brought about proved a very happy one for both parties. Fleming, however, wisely preserved silence as to the Hallowe'en trick which won him his bride.

Still another custom is Pricking the Egg. Take an egg, prick it with a pin and allow the white to drop into a wine-glass nearly filled with water. Take some of this in your mouth and go out for a walk. The first name you hear called aloud will be that of your future partner. An old woman solemnly assured the editor she had in her youthful days engaged in this Hallowe'en frolic, and the name of Archibald (her husband's name) " came up as it were from the very ground."

In addition to the foregoing, all of them connected with the Hallowe'en ceremonies, the Highlanders have the following decidedly eerie custom, which may be termed the summons of death. An individual goes to a public road which branches in three different directions. At the junction of these roads he seats himself on a three-legged stool on the eve of twelve o'clock; and as the hour strikes he hears proclaimed aloud the names of the several persons who will die in the parish before the next anniversary. Should the person carry along with him articles of wearing apparel, and throw an article away on the proclamation of each person's name, it will rescue that individual from his impending fate.

CHAPTER VI.

Carters' Plays at Liberton—Superstitions in connection with St. Catherine's Well—Old customs at Musselburgh—Riding the Marches again—Lanark and Linlithgow—The Polwarth Thorn—Gretna Green Marriages—Curious Land Tenure customs—Traditions regarding Macduff's Cross—Singular customs regarding Licensed Beggars in Scotland.

OLD CUSTOM AT LIBERTON.

THE only customs peculiar to Liberton were what were called "Carters' Plays." The carters had friendly societies for the purpose of supporting each other in old age, and in times of sickness. With the view partly of securing a day's recreation, and partly of recruiting their members and friends they used to have annual fêtes, when every man decorated his cart horse with flowers and ribbons, and a regular procession was formed, accompanied by a band of music, through this and some of the neighbouring parishes. To crown all, there was an uncouth race with cart-horses on the public road. The day's festivities ended in a dinner, for which a fixed sum was paid.

At St. Catherine's in this parish there is a famous well known as the *Balm Well:* Black oily substances continually float on the surface of its water. However many you may remove they still appear as numerous as before. In ancient times a sovereign virtue was supposed to reside in this well, and it was customary for persons afflicted with cutaneous complaints to partake of its waters. The nuns of the Sciennes made an annual pilgrimage to it in honour of St. Catherine. King James VI. visited it in 1617, and ordered it to be properly enclosed, and provided with a door and staircase, but it was destroyed and filled up by Cromwell's soldiers in 1650. It has again been opened and repaired, and is still in a state of preservation.

SHOOTING AT THE BUTTS.

When shooting at the "Butts" was a popular pastime in Scotland, the company of Archers at Edinburgh had a silver arrow presented to them by the Corporation of Musselburgh, to be shot for annually. The victor received £1 10s. and a dozen of claret from the town, and was bound to attach a medal of gold or silver to the arrow before the next year's annual meeting. This arrow had a series of such medals affixed to it from 1605 onwards, with the single exception of the memorable '45.

RIDING THE MARCHES AT MUSSELBURGH AND ELSEWHERE.

As in many other places, the ancient feudal system of "Riding the Marches," was observed here once in fifty years. The riders, seven incorporated trades, each headed by its captain, followed in the train of the magistrates and town council. This formidable cavalcade was preceded by the town officers with their ancient Brabant spurs, and a champion armed *cap-a-pie*. A gratuity was allowed to a minstrel who attended at the succeeding feast, and recited in verses the glories of the pageant. In "Scotland, Social and Domestic," which was published in 1869, Dr. Charles Rodgers writes that the burghs of Lanark and Linlithgow preserved this ancient practice with all the ceremony of former times. Though described elsewhere in connection with another locality, we may give the following as further illustrating this interesting ceremony. At the former place, after those who have joined in the diversions for the first time have been tumbled over and drenched in the "ducking-hole," the procession next marches to the plantations of Jerviswoode and Cleghorn, when the youths cut boughs from the birch trees, with which they proceed through the streets in boisterous mirth. They finally assemble at the Cross, where, under a statue reared to the memory of Wallace, they sing " Scots wha hae." The juvenile celebration terminates at noon. The magistrates and town council now appear at the Cross, attended by the town's drummer on horseback. A procession is formed, which, after inspecting the marches, enters the race-ground, then amidst demonstrations of merriment from the assembled multitude, a race is run for a pair of spurs. The proceedings terminate in a banquet in the County Hall.

The celebration at Linlithgow is similar in character to the above. The sovereign's health is drunk at the Cross, when the glasses are drained off they are tossed among the crowd. A procession is formed, the members of the Corporation seated in carriages take the lead. Then follow the trades bearing banners,—the farm-servants of the neighbourhood mounted and displaying from their bonnets a profusion of ribands, bring up the rear. After a march of several miles the procession returns to the Cross, whence the different bodies proceed to their favourite taverns to dedicate the evening to social mirth.

> "That ev'ry man might keep his owne possessions,
> Our fathers us'd in reverent processions
> (With zealous prayers, and with praisefull cheere),
> To walke their parish-limits once a yeare ;
> And well-knowne marks (which sacrilegious hands
> Now cut or breake) so bord'red out their lands,
> That ev'ry one distinctly knew his owne ;
> And many brawles, now rife, were then unknowne."

OLD CUSTOM AT POLWARTH.

The estate of Polwarth formerly belonged to Sinclair of Hermandston, whose family, so far back as the fifteenth century, terminated in co-heiresses. Out of their numerous suitors Marieta and Margaret Sinclair preferred the sons of their powerful neighbour, Home of Wedderburn. On the death of the young ladies' father they were taken care of by an uncle, who, anxious to prevent their marrying that he himself might heir their estates, immured them in his castle somewhere in Lothian. However, his fair captives contrived to get a letter transmitted to their lovers by means of an old beggar woman, and they were soon gratified by the sight of the gallant youths accompanied by a goodly band of Mersemen before the gate of their prison. Their uncle remonstrated and resisted in vain. His nieces were taken from him and carried off in triumph to Polwarth. They were speedily united in marriage to their lovers, and part of the nuptial rejoicings consisted in a merry dance round the thorn tree which then grew in the centre of the village.

The lands of Polwarth were thus divided between the two houses, and while George, the eldest son carried on the line of the Wedderburn family, Patrick was the founder of the branch afterwards enobled by the title of Marchmont.

In commemoration of so remarkable an affair, marriage parties danced round the " Polwarth thorn."

> " At Polwart on the Green
> If you'll meet me the morn
> When lasses do convene
> To dance around the thorn.
>
> " At Polwart on the Green
> Among the new mown hay
> With songs and dancing there
> We'll pass the heartsome day."

This custom, which continued in force for

several centuries, is now in disuse partly through the fall of the original tree. About fifty years ago, however, the party that attended a paying, or "Penny Wedding," danced round the little enclosure where formerly stood the familiar tree, to the tune of "Polwarth on the Green," having previously pressed into their service an old woman, about the last who had seen weddings thus celebrated, to show them the manner of the dance.

GRETNA GREEN MARRIAGES.

The parish of Gretna has long been famous in the annals of matrimonial adventures for the marriages of fugitive lovers from England which have been celebrated here. The persons who followed this irregular practice were impostors who had no right whatever to exercise any part of the clerical functions. The greatest part of the trade was monopolised by a man who was originally a tobacconist, named Paisley, and not a blacksmith, as was for some time supposed. In former times so great was the number of marriages solemnized here, that this traffic brought in an income of nearly a thousand per annum to the officiating parties—the form of ceremony when any such was made use of, was that of the church of Scotland. On these occasions, when the *person* happened to be intoxicated, which was not unfrequently the case, a certificate only was given. The following is a copy of one of those certificates in the original spelling :—

"This is to sartfay all persons that may be concerned, that A. B. from the parish of C. and in county of D., and E. F. from the parish of G. and in the county of H. both comes before me and declayred themselves to be single persons, and was mayried by the form of the Kirk of Scotland, and agreeble to the Church of England, and givine ondre my hand this 18th day of March, 1793."

Paisley's terms for tying the mystical knot varied according to the rank and circumstances of the parties who claimed his services. A *noggin* (two gills of brandy) sufficed as a fee from poor people. Curious to relate, this arch-imposter prosecuted his illegal trade for nearly half a century.

LAND TENURE CUSTOMS.

There are very many exceeding curious and interesting customs in Scotland in connection with land tenures. We give a few instances as illustrative of the subject in general. An ancient foot-race, in connection with Carnwath fair, forms one of the tenures by which the property of Carnwath is held by the Lockhart family. The prize was a pair of *red hose:* these were regularly contested for. In former years the laird used to have a messenger in readiness, whenever the race was finished, to communicate the intelligence to the Lord Advocate of Scotland.

The Barony of Pennicuik, the property of Sir George Clerk, Bart., is held by the following singular tenure: The proprietor is bound to sit upon a large rock, called the Buckstone, and wind three blasts of a horn when the king comes to hunt on the Borough Moor near Edinburgh. On account of this singular custom the family have adopted as their crest a demi-forester proper, winding a horn with the motto, *Free for a blast.*

The family of Morrison of Braehead in Midlothian, held their lands under the service of presenting a silver ewer, basin, and towel, for the king to wash his hands when he shall happen to pass the bridge of Cramond. The heir of Braehead discharged his duty at the banquet given to George the 4th, in the Parliament House in Edinburgh, in 1822.

The tenure by which the Sprotts of Urr hold their lands, is their presenting butter brose in King Robert's Bowl to any of the Kings of Scotland who happen to pass the Urr.

On a small island not far from Kilchurn Castle there are the remains of a ruined fortress. In 1267, this little demesne with its castle, and some adjoining lands were granted by King Alexander III., to Gilbert M'Naughten, the chief of the clan, on condition that he entertained the king whenever he passed that way.

The tenure by which the Marquis of Tweeddale holds his feus in Gifford, parish of Yester, is as follows—" Each feuar should attend the Marquis of Tweeddale the space of two days yearly sufficiently *mounted with horse and arms*, upon his own proper charges and expenses, when he sall be desired to do the samen;" also that he should attend other two days at the Marquis's expenses, " should ride at two fairs yearly at Gifford," and perform a day or days work yearly for winnowing of hay in the parks of Yester.

Tradition represents Macduff's Cross as erected in consequence of a privilege granted by Malcolm III., to his faithful friend Macduff, thane of Fife, to the effect that any one within the ninth degree of kindred to him who might commit a deadly crime should attain a sanctuary at this cross. When an individual claimed the privilege he was obliged to bring nine cows and bind them to as many rings in the pedestal of the cross, and also to wash himself free of the blood at a set of springs in the neighbourhood, known by the name of the nine wells.

BEGGING CUSTOMS.

The Poor Law has removed many ancient usages, but at no very remote period the magistrates and church session of Montrose met at a particular time of the year, and gave out badges to such as they knew to be under the necessity of begging. These licensed beggars went through the towns on the first of every month, but were not allowed to beg at any other time, nor could they go beyond the bounds of the parish. Fortunately, however, the good people of Montrose were so liberal in their donations to the applicants for aid that these did not require assistance from any public funds except when incapacitated from begging by sickness.

There formerly existed other mendicants, known as the " Gaberlunzie " or travelling beggar, and the King's Bedesmen or Blue Gowns. The number of this latter and higher class of privileged beggars corresponded with the years of the king's life. They received annually a cloak of coarse blue cloth, a pewter badge, and a leathern purse containing some " Pennies Sterling," the amount of which varied with the age of the sovereign. Sir Walter Scott, in his beautiful novel of the " Antiquary," introduces the reader to one of this venerable confraternity in the person of Edie Ochiltree.

CHAPTER VII.

Customs connected with St. Fillan's Well—Scottish Custom regarding May Dew—St. Serf's festival at Culross—Palm Sunday held at Lanark—Riding the marches at Lanark—Killing a sheep at Lanark-Old custom at Kelso—The King's Ease at Ayr—Burning the chaff after death—Creeling the Bridegroom in Berwickshire—Marriage customs and Superstitions in Invernesshire—Ancient customs at

Carluke—Scottish funeral customs—Horse-Racing in Scotland—Farmers Parade in Ayrshire—Shooting for the Silver Gun at Dumfries.

CUSTOMS CONNECTED WITH ST. FILLANS WELL.

ST. FILLAN'S well, like some others, was long believed to cure insanity, and the luckless sufferers received very rough handling to effect this, being thrown from a high rock down into the well, and then locked up for the night in the ruined chapel. On the witch elm that shades St. Fillan's spring, were hung the gay rags and scraps of ribbon wherein the saint was supposed to find delight—the average of two hundred patients were annually brought to this well. A very important feature in the ceremonial of St. Fillan's, Struthill, and other wells where lunatics were cured, is, that after their bath in the holy fountain and their surmise processions, they were tied to a pillar supposed to be far more ancient than the christian church wherein it stood. If next morning the patients were found loose the cure was esteemed perfect and thanks returned to the Saint. To this well the country women used to carry their weak and delicate children, and bathe them in the water, leaving some pieces of cloth hanging on the neighbouring bushes as a present or offering to Cella Fillan the tutelar saint of the parish. This custom was preserved until the middle of last century, when by the minister's command the well was filled up with stones.

SCOTTISH CUSTOM REGARDING MAY DEW.

Early on the morning of the first of May, young people used to go in parties to the fields to gather *May Dew*; to which some ascribed a happy influence and others a sort of medical virtue. Fair maidens might be seen tripping through the meadows before sun-rise, having been told by their elders " that if they got up in time to wash their faces with dew before the sun appeared they would have fine complexions for the remainder of the year."

ST. SERF'S FESTIVAL AT CULROSS.

St. Serf was considered as the tutelar saint of Culross (this place was at one time famous for its girdles), in honour of whom there was an annual procession on his day, viz. 1st July, early in the morning of which all the inhabitants, men and women, young and old, assembled and carried green branches through the town, decking the public places with flowers. The remainder of the day was devoted to festivity.

OLD CUSTOMS AT LANARK.

In the latest statistical History of Scotland, it is stated, that until the last thirty years Palm Sunday—probably the eve of that festival, was observed as a holiday at the Grammar School; and the scholar who presented the master with the largest candlemass offering, was appointed king and walked in procession with his life-guards and sergeants. The palm or its substitute, a large tree of the willow kind decked with a profusion of daffodils was carried before him; also a handsome embroidered flag, the gift of a lady residing in the town to the boys. The day finished off with a ball.

Another ancient custom, already described in connection with this place, was the Riding of the Marches on the Lammas or Landsmerk day. All persons who attended for the first time were ducked in the river Ususs, in the channel of which one of the march-stones is placed; and horse and fast races for a pair of spurs take place upon the moor. The burgh of Lanark from a very early date possessed an extensive and valuable piece of land in the neighbourhood, which in the old charters is designated *territorum burgi,* and it was the duty of the magistrates, burgesses, and freemen to perambulate the march of their territory, after which a report was drawn up stating that the March stones had been found in their ancient position ; this was signed by the witnesses, magistrates, and transmitted to the Exchequer. This custom is still kept up, although many modern innovations have crept into the ceremony. The Court who carries the Standard on the occasions of the processions, undoubtedly represents the person who, when the burgesses formed an important part of the armies of our earlier monarchs, was entrusted with the Banner of the burgh.* This custom is of Saxon origin, and was in all probability instituted here in or subsequent to the reign of Malcolm I.

Mr. Chambers, in his " Popular Rhymes of Scotland," gives the following amusing account of Lanark in the olden time. It is reported that the burgh of Lanark was in former days

---

* The " Upper Ward of Lanarkshire."

so poor, that the single flesher, of the town, who also exercised the calling of a weaver, in order to employ his spare time, would never dream of killing a sheep until he had received orders for the entire animal beforehand. Ere commencing the work of slaughter he would call on the minister, the Provost, and the town council, and prevail upon them to take shares. But if no purchaser appeared for the fourth quarter, the sheep received a respite until such could be found. The bellman, or *shallyman*, as he is called there, used to parade the streets of Lanark shouting aloud the following advertisement :—

>Bell-ell-ell
>There's a fat sheep to kill!
>A leg for the Provost
>And one for the priest.
>The Baillies and Deacons
>They'll take the neist ;
>And if the fourth leg we cannot sell
>The sheep it maun leeve and gae back
>Tae the hill.

OLD CUSTOMS AT KELSO.

Of the old Border games, foot-ball is the only one which is kept up with any degree of spirit. It was a long established practice for the Rector of the Grammar school and the other teachers in the town of Kelso to present "the king," that is the boy who made the most liberal Candlemas offering, with a football, which formed a source of amusement to the pupils for several weeks afterwards. The custom formerly connected with this game of the schools marching in procession through the town with a gilded ball on the top of a pole has long been abandoned.

THE KING'S EASE AT AYR.

In consequence of King Robert Bruce having experienced benefit from drinking the waters of a medicinal spring near the town of Ayr, when afflicted with a scorbutic disorder which in those days was styled leprosy, after ascending the throne he founded the priory of Dominican Monks, every one of whom was under the obligation of putting up prayers for his recovery, daily, and twice in holidays. After his death those masses were continued for the salvation of his soul.

King Robert likewise erected houses round the well—which after his recovery was called King's Ease or Case,—for the accommodation of eight lepers who were each allowed eight bolls of oat-meal, and 28s. Scotch money per annum. These donations were levied upon the lands, and are now laid upon the Duke of Portland. The farm of Shiels, in the neighbourhood of Ayr, was bound to give, if necessary, straw for the lepers' beds, also some to thatch their houses annually. Each leprous person had a drinking horn presented to him by the king, which continued to be hereditary in the house to which it was first granted. Out of compliment to Sir William Wallace, King Robert Bruce invested his descendants with the right of placing all the lepers upon the establishment of King's Ease. This patronage continued in the family of Craigie, till it was sold with the lands of the late Sir Thomas Wallace. The burgh of Ayr then purchased the right of applying the donation of King's Ease, to the support of the poor-house of Ayr.

BURNING THE CHAFF AFTER DEATH.

It was formerly a national custom for the relatives of the dead, the day after the funeral, to carry the chaff and bed-straw on which the person had died, to some hillock in the neighbourhood of the house and there burn them.

CREELING THE BRIDEGROOM IN BERWICKSHIRE.

The ancient matrimonial ordeal of creeling the bridegroom was observed at Eccles in a somewhat different way from other parishes. Once a year, or oftener, according to circumstances, all the men who had been married within the previous twelve months were creeled. With baskets, or creels, fastened on to their shoulders, they ran at full speed from their own houses to those of their nearest newly married neighbours, pursued by the unmarried men, who endeavoured to fill the baskets with stones, while the wives followed after with knives, striving to relieve them of their burdens by severing the ropes which attached the creels to their persons.

MARRIAGE CUSTOMS IN THE NORTH.

When a fisherman's marriage took place in the parish of Avoch the following superstitious practice was observed with a view, it was said, of thwarting the power of witchcraft. That was when the bridegroom's party arrived at the church door, the best man untied the shoe upon the left foot of the bridegroom, and formed a cross with a nail or a knife upon the right hand side of the door—the shoe remaining untied.

The fishermen were generally married at an early age, and seldom selected a bride above nineteen—The marriage was solemnised in the church on a Friday, but never before twelve o'clock. On one occasion, there were three marriages to take place on one day. The friends of the parties, according to custom waited upon the minister previously to engage his services. They were assured he should be in readiness and requested them to fix upon a convenient hour for the three parties to be married at once. The men looked grave, shook their heads, and said nothing. The minister entirely at a loss to understand this sudden gravity of countenance, the shaking of the heads, and the profound silence, begged them to explain their singular conduct. After some delay and hesitation upon their part, he was given to understand that were the three parties to be married at once, the consequences might be most serious, for there would be a struggle made by each party to get first out of the church, believing as they did that the party who contrived to be first would carry off the blessing. To prevent the contention that might take place under such circumstances, the minister offered to marry each party in succession. But next came the question of precedence, a delicate and difficult point at all times to settle, at least to every one's satisfaction, a point the deputies acknowledged they were quite unable to decide. This is not to be wondered at, considering that each party was anxious to be married first. After mature deliberation the minister thought fit to propose that the parties first contracted should be the first married, the proposal was unanimously agreed to, and the three couples were married on the Sunday following, in succession, especial care being taken that neither of the parties should meet the other on the way to and from the church, because it would be considered *unlucky*.

ANCIENT CUSTOMS AT CARLUKE.

Ancient customs and superstitions have rapidly disappeared in the parish of Carluke. About the middle of last century there might have been seen hanging in some byres a phial of Lee-Penny Water, to keep the cows from miscarriage in calving, and to prevent the milk from changing. To obtain the former of these objects, the barbarous custom of burying a live calf beneath the steps of the byre door was actually put into execution about that time by the servants of a respectable proprietor in the neighbourhood.

With regard to Lee-Penny water, the reputed talisman known as the Lee Penny is called so on account of its being set in the centre of a coin. This celebrated amulet was brought to this country by Sir Simon Lockhart of Lee, who accompanied the good Lord James Douglas to the Holy Land, and was believed to possess certain valuable properties. The Saracen lady from whom Sir Simon received the relic in part payment of her husband's ransom, acquainted him with the manner in which the amulet was to be used, and the uses to which it might be put, —the water in which it was dipped being reckoned, as she told him, to possess many medicinal virtues. The Lee Penny, since its arrival on Scottish shores has, it is said, wrought the most marvellous cures on man and beast, and has been sent for as far as from the northern counties of England. In the reign of Charles I. the people of Newcastle, when suffering from the plague, sent for and obtained a loan of it, depositing the sum of £6000 in its place as a pledge.

FUNERAL SERVICES.

The following orders were formerly observed in many parts of Scotland at the funerals of all persons who aimed at respectability of station. In "bidding to the buriall," no hour was mentioned, as ten in the morning was understood to be the time of assembling, and two or three in the afternoon as that of "lifting," and the intervening time was occupied in treating with "services" the various individuals as they arrived; these services being interspersed with admonitions, lengthened prayers and graces, when the mingled worship and entertainment terminated, the people proceeded to the churchyard after a scout stationed on a rising ground in the neighbourhood, gave intimation that no additional mourner was seen approaching the place of meeting. The following was the regular succession of the services:

1st Service—Bread and cheese with ale and porter.

2nd „ —Glass of rum with "burial bread."

3rd „ — Pipes filled with tobacco. To prepare the pipes was one of the duties of the women who sat at the late-wake.

4th   ,,   —Glass of port wine with cake.
5th   ,,   —Glass of sherry with cake.
6th   ,,   —Glass of whiskey.
7th   ,,   —Glass of wine not specified.
8th   ,,   —Thanks returned for the whole.

After which the service was renewed as soon as another individual made his appearance.

HORSE RACING IN SCOTLAND.

James IV. established horse-racing as a royal sport, and the first notice of horse-racing in Britain occurred in his reign. During the reign of Queen Mary, district horse races were began. In 1552 an annual horse race was established at Haddington and Lamington.

FARMERS' PARADE IN AYRSHIRE.

In former times the farmers' parade or race in the Lochwinnoch district was held on the first Tuesday of July. The horses were ranged according to their colours, with a captain at the head of each company, and the whole marched under the command of a colonel. The hats of the riders were adorned with ribbons, flowers, and newly shot oats, and some of them had showy sashes and other ornaments. The trappings of the horses were equally gaudy. One of the farmers carried a large flag, and they were accompanied by a piper or a band of instrumental music. Some of those who rode the fleetest steeds, after the parade was over, tried their speed in a horse race.

THE OLD CUSTOM AT DUMFRIES OF SHOOTING FOR THE SILLER GUN.

We are told, that when James I. went to Dumfries, he was so well pleased with his reception, that he presented to the town, a small model of a gun in silver, to be the object of a shooting match at periodical intervals, in imitation of some such sports, which were exhibited before him, on this occasion. The siller gun as it is called, has been since shot for every seven years, in much the same manner as silver arrows have been contended for, by archers at Musselburgh, Peebles, and St. Andrews. The place of sport, is a low holm by the side of the Nith, about a mile below the town, called the King's Holm. But this festival of the siller gun, has of late years been unpopular, from the number of accidents by which it is so disagreeably characterized. It unfortunately happens, that the important part of the festival, termed the "Drinking," is never postponed as it ought to be, till the termination of the sport, but diffused generally throughout its continuance. The consequence is, that the whole scene becomes one of riot and outrage. To show that people are not prevented from shooting when in a state of intoxication, a case is recorded of a man having once fired, when so overcome by liquor, that the gun was held for him by his friends, and yet he hit the mark, and was declared victor, though it was said, he was not aware of his good fortune, nor conscious of the honours that were paid him till next morning. In his ballad of the " Siller Gun," John Mayne has celebrated the annual commemoration of the festival. The following verses, are illustrative of the orgies practised on the occasion :

> "Louder grew the busy hum
> Of friends rejoicing as they come,
> Wi' double vis the drummers drum
> The pint stoups clatter,
> And bowls o' negus, milk, and rum
> Flew round like water."

CHAPTER VIII.

Interesting Hand-ball custom in Perthshire—Old custom in connection with Scottish Coronations—The Game of Shinty at Roseneath—Playing Football on Sunday—Christmas Sports in Aberdeenshire—Festive Games at Cullen—Marriage and Funeral Customs at Knockando—Superstitious customs in connection with the Dhu Loch—The Well of Loretta at Musselburgh—Chapman's Festival at Preston—Cock-fighting at Westruther—The Wapinshaw at Perth—Horse-racing at Perth in Olden Times—The Mount of Peace—Holy Wells at Muthill.

INTERESTING HAND BALL CUSTOM IN PERTHSHIRE.

AN annual custom used to prevail at Scone, for the bachelors and married men, to draw themselves up at the Cross of Scone, on opposite sides. A ball was then thrown up, and they played from the hour of two until sunset. The game was played after this fashion. The person who succeeded in catching the ball ran with it till overtaken by one or more of the opposite party. If able to shake himself free from his captors he ran on. If not he threw the ball from him, unless it was wrested out of his hands. No person was allowed to kick it. The object of the married men was to hang the ball, *i.e.*, to put it three times in a hole in the moor—the *dool* or limit on the one hand. That of the bachelors was to drown it, *i.e.*, to dip it three times in a deep pool in the river—the boundary on the other. The party who could achieve this feat won the game. If neither party proved victorious the ball was cut equally asunder at sunset. This custom is supposed to have originated in the days of chivalry. An Italian is said to have come into this part of the country challenging all the parishes, which were to undergo a certain penalty should they decline his challenge. Scone was the only one that accepted it. Proving victorious, in commemoration of their victory, the game was substituted. Whilst the custom continued every man in the parish, the gentlemen not excepted, was obliged to be out and support the side to which he belonged; and the person who neglected to perform his duty on that occasion had to submit to a fine. This custom being attended with some inconveniences, it was abandoned many years ago.

OLD CUSTOM IN CONNECTION WITH SCOTTISH CORONATIONS.

Between sixty and seventy yards north from the eminence where the ancient Scottish kings were crowned at Scone, is a place vulgarly called Boot Hill. It is likewise called, Omnis Terra, or, every man's land. The tradition of the people of the parish, concerning Boot Hill, is, that at the coronation of a king, every man who assisted brought so much earth in his boots, that each might see the king crowned on his own land; and that afterwards, they cast the earth out of their boots upon this hill, whereby it obtained the name of Boot Hill, and Omnis Terra.

THE GAME OF SHINTY AT ROSENEATH.

In the prettily situated parish of Roseneath, Dumbartonshire, New Year's day was anciently observed with great festivities. For weeks previously, the youths of the district, prepared for the grand annual game of shinty. And in one of the fields adjoining the church, hundreds of people assembled with music and banners, either to witness, or to join in the contest.

PLAYING FOOTBALL ON SUNDAY.

In the good old times, the parishioners of

Menzie, were in the habit of assembling upon the green on Sunday morning, to play at football. On these occasions, their clergyman, Mr. Chalmers, who experienced great difficulty in getting his people to attend church, occasionally took part with them in the game. He thus gained their affections, and in a short time, prevailed upon them to attend him to church, and to listen to his instructions.

CHRISTMAS SPORTS IN ABERDEENSHIRE.

At Yule-tide, the Strathdonians, observed the festive season, with prize-shootings, and subscription dances. These were generally got up for charitable purposes. They were set on foot for the relief of some case of poverty, or distress in the neighbourhood; and thus, at the cost of a few pence to each individual, a large sum was raised for the benefit of the needy family. Another charitable custom prevailed. When any singular and melancholy case of distress occurred, the young men in this parish, assembled together, and, frequently accompanied by music, went to each house, where they received a donation, either of food or money.

Formerly football was a favourite amusement with persons of every age in the parish of Monymusk; and parties came from other districts to take part in it. "The Monymusk Christmas ba-ing," with its various mischances has been celebrated in a humorous poem, by the Rev. John Skinner, Grandfather of the present Bishop of Aberdeen.

> " The hurry-burry now began
>   Was right weel worth the seeing,
> Wi' routs and raps frae man to man
>   Some getting and some gieing.
> And a' the tricks o' fut and hand
>   That ever was in being ;
> Sometimes the ba' a yirdlins ran,
>   Sometimes in air was fleeing
>   Fu' heigh that day.
> . . . . . .
> How ne'er in Monymusk been seen
>   Sae mony weel-beft skins ;
> Of a' the ba'men there was nane
>   But had twa bloody shins ;
> Wi' strenzied shutters many ane
>   Dree'd penance for their sins,
> And what was warst, scouped hame at e'en
>   May be to hungry inns
>   And cauld that day.

FESTIVE GAMES AT CULLEN.

At the winter festivals of Hallowe'en, Christmas, and other holidays at Cullen, the younger portion of the community used to resort to the sands and links of the Bay of

Cullen, for the purpose of playing football, running races, throwing the hammer, playing bowls, etc. They left the town in procession preceded by the pipes and other music, and were attended by numbers from the adjacent districts. These games were keenly contested, and the victor was crowned with a bonnet adorned with feathers and ribbons, previously prepared by the ladies. At the conclusion of the games the whole party danced on the green with great merriment. After which the procession was again formed, and returned to the town, the victor, preceded by the music, leading the way. A ball took place in the evening, at which he presided, with the privilege of wearing his bonnet and feather. The bowls were played by rolling or throwing a cannon ball, and he who could with the fewest strokes send it beyond a mark at the further end of the link, was declared the victor. A man being on one occasion killed while playing at this game, the magistrates caused it to be discontinued.

The ancient festivities of Harvest Home, Hallowe'en, and Brose-day, were formerly observed in the above-mentioned parish. Here the farmers carefully preserved their cattle against witchcraft by placing boughs of the mountain ash, and honeysuckle, within cowhouses on the second of May. They hoped to preserve the milk of their cows, and their wives from miscarriage, by tying red threads* round them. They bled the supposed witch to preserve themselves from her charms. They visited the wells of Spey and Dracholdy when afflicted with disease, offering small pieces of money, etc.

MARRIAGE AND FUNERAL CUSTOMS AT KNOCKANDO.

One of the customs at Knockando was for the married women generally to retain their maiden names in preference to assuming those of their husbands. Another strange custom was that the father, who should attend as chief mourner, was seldom present at the

---

* Miss Gordon Cumming tells us that in Banffshire it is still a common practice to tie a couple of twigs crosswise with red thread and place them above the door of the cowhouse; and that "various knowing old wives," keep a red thread twisted round the tail of their cow, as a safeguard from evil. Also that this reverence for a scarlet twine is by no means confined to these isles; that the witches of Mongolia carry on their incantations by the means of scarlet silken thread, and that Vishnu protected some of his votaries from the sorceries of the demon-worshippers by tying threads on their arms.

funeral of his eldest child. Tuesdays, Thursdays, and Saturdays, were the common days for weddings to take place; the common people having some superstitious notions regarding Mondays and Fridays.

CUSTOMS IN CONNECTION WITH THE DOW LOCH.

There used to be a small Loch called the Dow, Dhu, or Black Loch, which was reputed to possess extraordinary virtue in the healing of diseases. It seems to have been looked upon as a perpetual Bethesda, for its waters were reputed to be efficacious in the cure of every disease, but especially of cattle subjected to the spells of witchcraft. It was not necessary that the person ailing should himself visit the loch. A deputy was employed, who had to obey certain rules. He had to carry a part of the dress of the invalid, or of the furniture of the person bewitched as an offering to the spirit of the loch. When the messenger reached Dow Loch, he had to draw water in a vessel which had never touched the ground, to turn himself round with the sun, and to throw his offering to the spirit over his left shoulder—formalities all indicative of Druidical origin. In carrying the water away to the sick person or animal, the messenger may not look back, and, like the prophet's servant, the man was to salute no person by the way.

In the days of superstition great virtue was attached to water drawn from under a bridge along which the living walked and the dead were carried.

LOCH TORRIDON.

In a churchyard on Loch Torridon there is a well where, it used to be said, from time immemorial three stones have been perpetually whirling round and round. All kinds of sickness and disease have been cured by carrying one of these stones in a bucket of water to the invalid, who was only required to touch the stone to be restored to health. Its mission accomplished, the Talisman was restored to its place, when it commenced whirling as before. But, alas! one of these healing stones now lies quietly at the bottom of the well, refusing any longer to whirl like the others, simply because a woman, great in her faith, once took it home with her to perform a cure on her sick goat.

HOLY WELL AT MUSSELBURGH.

The long celebrated chapel dedicated to Our Lady of Loretto, stood beyond the eastern gate of Musselburgh, in Midlothian, on the margin of the links. But we have no authentic accounts as to the time of its erection. Pilgrimages from all parts of Scotland were performed to this shrine, which was connected, it is supposed, with the Nunnery of Sciennes, in the northern district of Edinburgh. Expectant mothers sent handsome presents of money accompanying their child-bed linen, which latter was consecrated, for a good fee, to promote their safe delivery and recovery. The celebrity of this place was increased by a hermit, who inhabited a cell adjoining the chapel. So successful was he believed to be in the performance of miracles, that, at the commencement of the sixteenth century, it was esteemed the most noted shrine in Scotland. King James V. performed a pilgrimage from Stirling to it, ere he sailed for France, to woo and win his future queen. The materials of the discredited and ruined chapel, are said to have been the first belonging to any sacred edifice after the Reformation, devoted to any secular purpose. They were employed in the erection of the present town gaol. For this piece of sacrilege, it is said, the inhabitants of

Musselburgh were annually excommunicated at Rome, till the end of the last century.

CHAPMAN'S FESTIVAL AT PRESTON.

At Preston, in a garden on the opposite side of the road from the castle gardens, stands the ancient village cross. Annually at the beginning of July, it was formerly the scene of much innocent mirth and merry-making. As if in obedience to some enchanter's wand, a large crowd suddenly encircled the solitary pillar, and exchanged friendly greetings and good wishes. This was doubtless a continuation of some ancient custom; and as this cross is, or was, the property of the chapmen (pedlars) of the Lothians, having been acquired by them in olden times, it is supposed by some antiquarians that the company referred to, were representatives of that ancient and respectable fraternity. The so styled chapman was in former times a most useful member of society. In the country districts, when roads were bad, towns distant, and means of communication with them rare, his appearance was generally greeted with delight. The better class of these itinerant merchants pursued their journeys on horseback, conveying their merchandise on pack saddles. The chapman or pedlar, is not now so frequently met with in Scotland.

COCK-FIGHTING AT WESTRUTHER.

In the days of cock-fighting, and other equally barbarous sports, the school-boys of Westruther were accustomed to amuse themselves with cock-fighting on Fastern's eve—each bringing a cock trained for the purpose, and the victor in the conquest had, besides the honour of the conquest, the burden imposed upon him of paying for a football, which ended the sport of the day. This barbarous amusement with which Fastern's eve was ushered in, was discontinued about 1840. The more innocent football game, so closely connected with it, was also gradually relinquished. The matches often consisted of more than an hundred on each side. Sometimes the whole parish turned out, but generally the battle was fought between the married and unmarried men. There used to be also much sport and merriment in Westruther, at the celebrations of Penny Weddings, but these on the interference of the Church Courts, were prohibited. At the beginning of last century, cock-fighting was a favourite pastime both with old and young. Even children took part in it. The Duke of York, it is said, introduced it into Scotland in 1683. Towards the close of the 17th century, this barbarous practice had become so popular and engrossing, that in 1704, the Town Council of Edinburgh interfered to prevent it, as it was fast becoming an impediment to business.

THE WAPINSHAW AT PERTH.

From the City Records of Perth it appears that the Wapinshaw was from an early period observed in Perth according to statute. The magistrates by beat of drum and proclamation called out the weaponshawers to exercise on the North Inch, at the fixed periods or sometimes oftener. They appointed a captain and other officers, and gave them an ensign which was called the *hangenzier*, the bearer of which was styled the hangenzier-bearer. At particular times the distinguished banner having upon it the Holy Lamb *en passant* was produced. Absentees were fined 40s. each. After the year 1620, there is no account of weaponshawing in Perth.

HORSE-RACING CUSTOM AT PERTH.

Horse-racing appears to have existed in the Fair City from an early period. The place appropriated to it was the South Inch; the course was marked by six stakes. The first account given of a prize being run for is in 1613, this was a silver arrow given by Ninian Graham of Garvock, in the name of John Graham of Bogside. In 1631, there were three prize silver bells, but they were declared to be unsuitable, and a cup was substituted in their place, which weighed more than eight ounces. Till 1688, the race was called "the bell race," by authority of the magistrates, it was afterwards referred to as a "race for a cup and other prizes."

BELL-RINGING CUSTOM AT PERTH.

"In the month of February, 1586-7, the Perth Session ordains Nicol Balmain to ring the Curfew and workman bell in the morning and evening the space of ane quarter of an hour at the times appointed, viz. four hours in the morning, and eight at even," and in the town's record, 1657, is "an act requiring obedience to the ringing of bells for *putting out fires.*"

OLD CUSTOM AT FOWLIS WESTER.

In the parish of Fowlis Wester there is a

Si'un, which signifies in Gaelic a *mount of peace*. On the Si'uns the Druids held assizes when it was customary to kindle a large bonfire called *Saurhin* or the fire of peace. On Hallow even, a Druidical festival, these fires are still lighted up in this district, and are said to retain the same name.

St. Methvenmas market is held at Fowlis annually on the 6th November. This was in former times the festival of the parish, and the anniversary of the saint to whom the church was dedicated at its consecration, when the people constructed booths to indulge in hospitality and mirth; it also became a commercial mart, and assumed the name of *ferial* or holy day. Many of our ancient fairs have a similar origin.

HOLY WELL CUSTOMS AT MUTHILL.

The parish of Muthill at one time contained several springs or wells much esteemed for their virtues, real or imaginary. The one at Straid, in the district of Blair-in-nan, was much frequented, as it was esteemed effectual in curing the hooping-cough. In the course of this century a family came from Edinburgh, a distance of nearly sixty miles, to have the benefit of the well. The water must be drunk before sunrise or immediately after it sets, and that out of a "quick cow's horn," or a horn taken from a live cow. In the same district is St. Patrick's well, so named from a chapel once there, and probably dedicated to this saint. It is not known what connection St. Patrick had with this sequestered spot, but it is certain that formerly the inhabitants held his memory in such veneration, that on his day neither the clap of the mill was heard nor the plough seen to move in the furrow. A third well upon the side of the Machony was of still greater importance. It was called the well of Strathill, and was most sought after by the credulous, as its waters were deemed effectual in curing madness. In 1668 several persons testified before the presbytery of Stirling, that having carried a woman thither, "they had stayed two nights at a house near to the well; that the first night they did bind her twice to a stone at the well but she came into the house to them being loosed without any help. The second night they bound her again to the same stone, and she returned loose. And they declare also, she was very mad before they took her to the well, but since that time she is working and sober in her wits." This well long retained its former celebrity, and votive offerings were cast into it in the year 1723.

CHAPTER IX.

Marriage and Funeral customs at Pettie—The Duke of Perth and the Crieff fair—Fairy doings in Inverness-shire—Curious marriage custom at Ardersier—Superstitious customs at Fodderty—The old Scottish game of curling—Farmers custom at Elgin—Happy and unhappy feet—Funeral customs at Campsie—Gool Riding in Perthshire.

OLD CUSTOMS AT PETTIE.

FORMERLY it was customary when marriages took place in the church of Pettie for the children of the parish school to barricade the door, and refuse admittance to the party till the bridegroom should either make a present of fourpence to buy a new football, or earn exemption from the custom by kicking the old ball over the church. If the would-be benedict could not achieve the exploit of kicking the ball, and would not pay the pence, the cleverest fellow, might take off the bride's shoes, and, thus degraded, the bridegroom was allowed to enter the church.

At funerals also it was a custom peculiar to this parish to run as fast as possible, so that often persons fell when carrying the body to the grave. Hence in the neighbouring parishes, if rain came on, or if it was wished to quicken the progress of a funeral, it used to be said, "let us take the Pettie step to it." This custom was revived some time ago by the youngsters of the parish at the funeral of a woman known as *Camranach-na-peasanach's* wife, and who had been dreaded and consulted as a witch. Other times other manners, the Pettie step at funerals is now as decorous as that of their neighbours, and the school impost at marriages no longer exists.

OLD FAIR CUSTOM AT CRIEFF.

In past days, the principal fairs held at Crieff were opened with considerable pomp by the Duke of Perth in person. He held his courts, often in the open air, in the town, and afterwards rode through the market at the head of his guard, and proclaimed his titles at the different marches or boundaries of his property. Many of the feuars were bound by their charters to provide a given number of halbert-men that composed the guard at these fairs, and it was only in later times that their services were dispensed with.

FAIRY DOINGS IN INVERNESS-SHIRE.

At no very distant period, a belief in fairies and their gambols, existed in Ardersier, Inverness-shire. About 1730, it is said, a man of the name of Munro had a sickly attenuated child, which he and his neighbours considered to be a changeling, substituted by the sportive elves, at an unguarded moment, in place of his own. There is a conical knoll in the carse called *Tom Earnais*, or Henry's Knoll, which was famed as the scene of the moonlight revels of Titania and her court; and it was believed, that if the changeling were left overnight on the hillock, the real child would be found in its stead in the morning. The infatuated father actually subjected his ailing offspring to this ordeal, and in the morning found it a corpse.

CURIOUS MARRIAGE CUSTOM AT ARDERSIER.

The fishermen here marry at an early age, and generally before they acquire the means of furnishing a house, even with the most necessary articles. To compensate in some measure for the deficency, the custom of *thrigging*, as it is called, was adopted by the young wife, a few days after marriage. She, accompanied by her bridesmaid, visited her neighbours and friends, and they each presented her with some little article of house plenishing, generally a piece of earthenware, usage permitting the visitors to choose what article she pleased.

SUPERSTITIOUS CUSTOMS AT FODDERTY.

There is a small spring, which rises in a circular hollow in a solid rock, in the west side of Rhoagie, called *Tobar-na-doushunich*, the water of which was believed to possess the virtue of indicating whether a sick person shall survive or not. It was taken from the spring before sunrise; and, after the patient had been bathed or immersed in it, if the water appeared of a pure colour, it foretold recovery; but if of a brown mossy colour, it betokened death. Many years ago, a mother brought her sickly child, a distance of thirty miles, to the spring. On approaching it, she was startled by the appearance of an animal with glaring eye-balls, leaping into it. The poor mother considered this as a fatal omen. Her affection, however, for her offspring overcame her fears. She dislodged the creature, and bathed her child, after which it slept more soundly than it had ever done before. This seemed to confirm the healing virtues of the well, but the child did not long survive. Within the same period, two friends of a parishioner whose life was despaired of, went to consult the spring in his behoof, and to fetch some of the water. On placing the pitcher in it, the water assumed a circular motion from south to west. They returned with joy, and told the patient that there was no cause to fear, as the motion of the water being, from south to west, was a sure indication that he would recover, whereas, had it been from north to west, he must have died. The person recovered.

THE OLD GAME OF CURLING.

The ancient and popular game of curling, is supposed to be of Continental origin, and that it was introduced into this country by those Flemish emigrants who settled in Scotland, towards the close of the fifteenth century. As St. Andrews is the headquarters of golf, so is Edinburgh the headquarters of curling; and it was formerly customary for the magistrates of the Modern Athens, to head a procession to Duddingstone Loch, when the weather was such as to permit of a contest on the ice. In certain districts, females used to take part in the game. At Lamington, in Lanarkshire, the married women frequently matched themselves against the spinsters, and the scientific zeal and skill with which both parties pursued their pastime, created much amusement amongst the bystanders. Curling is played as follows: The curlers range themselves into two opposing parties, and stand opposite to each other. They slide from one mark to another, large stones, of several pounds weight, of a round form, and furnished with wooden handles. The aim of the player is, to lay his stone as close to the mark as possible, and in doing so, to strike away the best placed of his opponents. Each curler is provided with a broom, in order to sweep away the snow, or any other impediment from the ice.

FARMERS' CUSTOM AT ELGIN.

In the middle of June, many of the farmers at Elgin, formerly went round their corn with burning torches, in honour of the *Cerealia*. At the full moon in March, they cut withes off the mistletoe or ivy, made circles of them, kept them all year, and pretended to cure illness with them. At marriages and baptisms, they made a procession round the church with the sun, because the sun was the immediate object of the Druids' worship.

HAPPY AND UNHAPPY FEET.

Friday at Forglen in Banffshire used to be considered a very unlucky day on which to be married. The expressions, " happy and unhappy feet," were made use of by the inhabitants in the interchange of good and bad wishes. Thus, they wished a newly married couple "happy feet," and as a preventive to misfortunes of any kind, they saluted each other by kissing when they chanced to meet on the road to and from the church.

FUNERAL CUSTOMS AT CAMPSIE.

It was formerly the custom in the Campsie district, when the head of a family died, to invite all the inhabitants to attend the funeral. The visitors were served seated on boards in the barn, and by way of commencement were supplied with ale, then followed whisky, after this came shortbread, then some other kind of liquor, then a piece of currant bread, and a third supply either of whisky or wine. After this came bread and cheese, pipes and tobacco. This feast was called a service; sometimes it was repeated, in which case it was called a double service. However distant any part of the parish was from the place of interment, it was customary for the attendants to carry the coffin on hand-spokes. The mode of invitation was by a special messenger. This was styled "bidding to the funeral." No person was invited by letter. The form of words used were,—"You are desired to come to ——'s funeral to-morrow against ten o'clock." Although asked for that early hour the funeral never took place until the evening. It was customary for them to have two *Lyke-wakes*, when the young friends and neighbours watched the corpse. These were merry or sorrowful according to the position or rank of the deceased.

THE CUSTOM OF GOOL RIDING.

Unfortunately for the former inhabitants of Cargill, Perthshire, the fields in this parish were formerly over-run by a weed with a yellow flower called "gool," which grew amongst the grain especially in wet seasons, and greatly injured the corn, not only while growing, but during the winnowing of it. Such was the destruction caused by this noxious weed that it became absolutely necessary to adopt some effectual method for getting rid of it. Accordingly an act of the Barons' Court was passed imposing a fine of 3s. 4d. or a wedder sheep, on every tenant for each stock of gool that should be found growing amongst the corn on a particular day, and certain persons called gool-riders were appointed to ride through the fields searching for gool. Wherever it was found the fine was vigorously exacted.

CHAPTER X.

Old Customs at Kirkmichael—The Pedlars Tournament at Leslie—Superstitious custom at St. Monance—The Touch Hills—The Maiden Feast in Perthshire—The Society of Chopmen at Dunkeld—Announcement of Death at Hawick—The customs in connection with Nicknames—Religious custom on the approach of Death—Riding the Marches at Hawick—Scottish Masonic customs—Candlemas customs.

OLD CUSTOMS IN BANFFSHIRE.

ALTHOUGH quite unable to furnish any reason for their superstitious observances, the inhabitants of the parish of Kirkmichael, Banffshire, were formerly the slaves of times and seasons. The moon in her increase, full-growth, and decline, was with them the emblem of a rising, flourishing, and declining fortune. While in the wane they refused to engage in any important business, such as marriage, etc., but when in the two former stages of her revolutions, whatever was the nature of the undertakings in which they were employed, they predicted for themselves a successful issue. They had customs for Hallowe'en and the first night of the New Year. On the latter evening they were attentive observers of the weather. According as it was calm or boisterous, and as the wind blew, they prognosticated the nature of the weather they would have till the end of the year.

THE PEDLARS' TOURNAMENT.

The green of Leslie was in former years the theatre of annual sports of a rather ludicrous nature. The chief if not sole performers in these rural pastimes were the honourable fraternity of pedlars or packmen, who, by tilting at a ring, with wooden spears, on horseback, endeavoured hard, to imitate the chivalrous knights of old. Much merriment was excited whenever these doughty pedlars —their horses at full stretch—missed striking the ring, which, unfortunately for their composure, was but too often the case ; as it inevitably followed that the circumstance caused them to drop both reins and spears, and cling convulsively to their saddles. At these times the appearance presented by these modern Quixotes was in the highest degree ludicrous.

SUPERSTITIOUS CUSTOM AT ST. MONANCE.

The ancient bell which formerly rung the good people of St. Monance to church, and which hung suspended from a tree in the churchyard, was, strange to say, removed every year from that position during the herring season, the fishermen entertaining the superstitious belief that the fish were scared away from the coast by its noise. No compliment this to the sounds produced by the bell in question.

PILGRIMAGE TO ST. CORBET'S WELL.

At the summit of the Touch Hills, Stirlingshire, a little to the west of Stirling, there may be seen by the curious a crystal well which in ancient times was believed to possess the peculiar quality of insuring for a twelvemonth, the lives of all who drank of its waters, before sunrise on the first Sunday in May. In 1840 there were old men and women then alive who in their younger days had been of the number of those who made annual pilgrimages to St. Corbet's Well on the morning in question. They described the gatherings on the anniversaries as having been splendid. Husbands and wives, lovers with their sweethearts, young and old, grave and gay, crowded the hill tops in the vicinity of the well long before dawn, and each party on their arrival took copious draughts of the singularly blessed water. It is reported that St. Corbet, after a lapse of years, deprived the well of its life-preserving qualities in consequence of the introduction of "mountain dew" of a less innocent nature into these annual festivals.

THE MAIDEN FEAST.

In some parts of Perthshire it was till very lately the custom to give what was called a Maiden Feast, upon the finishing of the harvest; as a preparation for which the last handful of corn reaped in the field was called the Maiden. It was generally so contrived that this fell into the hands of one of the prettiest girls in the field; it was then decked up with ribbons, and brought home in triumph to the sound of bagpipes and fiddles. A good dance was given to the reapers, and the evening was devoted to merriment. Afterwards the "Maiden" was dressed out, generally in the form of a cross, and hung up, with the date attached to it in some conspicuous part of the house.

CHAPMEN AT DUNKELD.

The Society of Chapmen or itinerant merchants was a very ancient institution. The original charter was from James V. The general annual meeting of the Society was held alternately at Dunkeld and Coupar Angus. The meeting was styled a *Court*. All members coming to the market were obliged to attend it. They were summoned by one of the office-bearers, who, to enforce their attendance, went round to the different booths in open market, and took from each a piece of goods, or 2s. 6d., as a pledge for the owner's appearance. Each member was obliged to produce his weights and measures, which were compared with standards, kept for the purpose. After the court, the members dined together, and spent the evening in some public competition of dexterity or skill. Of these, Riding at the Ring, an amusement of ancient and warlike origin, and already referred to on a previous page, was the chief. Two perpendicular posts were erected on this occasion, with a cross beam, from which was suspended a small ring. The competitors were on horseback, each bearing a pointed rod in his hand, and he, who at full gallop, passed between the posts, carrying away the ring on his rod, gained the prize.

> " He was a braw gallant
>   And he rode at the ring ;
>   And the bonnie Earl Murray
>   He was fit to be a king."
>
> Old Ballad.

OLD CUSTOM AT HAWICK.

On the event of a death occurring in the parish of Hawick, it was formerly the custom for one of the burgh officers to proceed through the different districts of the town, ringing his bell, and intimating the death; which intimation was accompanied by a general invitation to the funeral. The bell was then taken to the house of mourning, and placed on the bed where the dead body lay, and in a position from which it was deemed sacrilegious to remove it, until the time appointed for the interment.

CUSTOMS REGARDING NICKNAMES.

At one time the strange custom prevailed all over Scotland, of distinguishing individuals by other than their proper names. This custom was at one time exceedingly common and was probably adopted in ancient times for the purpose of drawing a broader line of distinction between persons, who, belonging to the same class and bearing the same names, could not, but for this method, be easily distinguished the one from the other. It is not a little singular that these designations have been handed down from father to son in regular succession through the course of many generations. Indeed there are some old people who have been so long accustomed to this singular fashion that their proper names are but seldom used, and remain quite unknown to many of their neighbours. Even in the Register of Deaths, where, one would imagine, the evidences of such a strange custom were least likely to be traced, there is actually a faithful record of the soubriquets by which the ancestors of the present generation were commonly distinguished.

BURYING WITHOUT A COFFIN.

It was customary in some parts of Scotland to employ only one coffin in the interment of paupers. This by all accounts, was used merely for the purpose of conveying the corpses to their final resting place, and was so constructed as to be capable of opening by a hinge underneath, by which means the body was permitted to escape when lowered into the grave.

RELIGIOUS CUSTOM ON THE APPROACH OF DEATH.

The following custom long prevailed in many places. When any member of a family was considered to be dying, the apartment was not only frequented by relations and neighbours, but in many instances, the entire company united in religious worship, selecting one of the psalms most suited to the occasion, such as the twenty-third, the forty-third, or the hundred and eighteenth. This they sang with a low and solemn melody, while the soul of the dying person was passing into the world of spirits. And then, when the mortal struggle appeared to be over, it was succeeded by a song of triumph and of praise, consisting not frequently of a portion of the hundred and seventh psalm.

RIDING THE MARCHES AT HAWICK.

The ceremonies observed in the parish of Hawick at the riding of the marches, were pretty similar to those engaged in, at other places. The honour of carrying the standard of the town, the original of which is said to have been taken from the English after the battle of Flodden, devolved upon the Cornet, a young man previously selected for the purpose.

The following are a few verses from an ancient song, which was sung by the Cornet and his attendants, from the roof of an old tenement belonging to the town.

> "We'll a' hie to the moor a-riding,
> Drumlanrig gave it for providing
> Our ancestors of martial order
> To drive the English off our Border.

> "At Flodden field our fathers fought it,
> And honour gain'd though dear they bought it,
> By Teviot side they took this colour—
> A dear memorial of their valour.

> "Though twice of old our tower was burned,
> Yet twice the foemen back we turned,
> And ever should our rights be trod on,
> We'll face the foe on Tirioden.

> "Up wi' Hawick its rights and common,
> Up wi' a' the Border bowman!
> Tiribus and Tirioden,
> We are up to guard the common."

SCOTTISH MASONIC CUSTOMS.

The eve of St. John is a great day amongst the masonic lodges of Scotland. What takes place at Melrose may be considered a fair example of the whole. Immediately after the election of office-bearers for the ensuing year the brethren walk in procession three times round the cross, and afterwards dine together under the presidency of the newly elected Grand Master. About six in the evening the members again turn out and form into line two abreast, each bearing a lighted flambeau, and decorated with their peculiar emblems and insignia. Headed by the heraldic banners of the Lodge, the procession performs the same route three times round the cross and thus proceed to the Abbey. On these occasions the crowded streets present a scene of the most animated description. The joyous strains of a well conducted band, the waving torches, and incessant showers of fireworks make the scene a carnival. But at this time the venerable Abbey is the chief point of attraction and resort; and as the mystic torchbearers thread their way through its mouldering aisles and round its massive pillars, the outlines of its gorgeous ruins become singularly illuminated and brought into bold and striking relief. The whole extent of the Abbey is, with measured step and slow, gone three times round. But when near the finale, the whole masonic body gather to the chancel, and forming one grand semi-circle round it where the heart of King Robert Bruce lies deposited, near the high altar, and the band strikes up the patriotic air, " Scots wha ha'e wi' Wallace bled," the effect produced is overpowering. Midst showers of rockets and glare of blue lights the scene closes, the whole reminding one of some popular Saturnalia held in a monkish town during the middle ages.

OLD CANDLEMAS CUSTOMS.

There was a curious custom of old standing in Scotland in connexion with Candlemas Day. On that day it was lately a universal custom in some parts of the country for the children attending school to make small presents of money to their teachers. The master sits at his desk or table exchanging for the moment his usual authoritative look for one of bland civility, and each child goes up in turn and lays the offering down before him the sum being generally apportioned to the abilities of the parents. Sixpence or a shilling were the most common sums in many schools, but some gave half and whole crowns and even more. The boy and girl who gave most were respectively styled King and Queen. The children being then dismissed for a holiday proceed along the streets in a confused procession carrying the King and Queen in state exalted upon a seat formed of crossed hands which probably from this circumstance is called the King's chair. In some schools it used to be customary for the teacher on the conclusion of the offerings to make a bowl of punch, and each urchin was regaled with a glass to drink the King and Queen's health, and a biscuit. The latter part of the day was generally devoted to what was called a *Candlemas bleeze* or blaze, namely, the conflagration of any piece of furze which might exist in their neighbourhood, or, were that wanting, of an artificial bonfire.

An old popular custom in Scotland on Candlemas day was to hold a football match the east end of the town against the west, the married men against the unmarried, or one parish against another. The Candlemas

Ba' as it was called brought the whole community out in a state of great excitement. On one occasion not long ago when the sport took place in Jedburgh, the contending parties after a struggle of two hours in the Jed, fought it out amidst a scene of fearful splash and dabblement to the infinite amusement of a multitude looking on from a bridge.

CHAPTER XI.

Strange custom at Kirkmaiden—Singular obituary announcement at Bo'ness—Holy well observances in Kincardineshire—Ancient races at Kilmarnock—Creeling the Bridegroom again— Old Border customs—Alarm signals—The right hand unbaptised—The fiery peat—Good faith of the Borderers—Sunday dissipation—Punishment of matrimonial infidelity in former times—Riding the stang—Marriage processions—Odd football custom at Foulden—Strange holy well superstitions—Curious customs with regard to fishing—The silver gun of Kirkcudbright.

STRANGE CUSTOM AT KIRKMAIDEN.

THERE is a small cave at Kirkmaiden, Wigton-shire, on the south-east between the buoys of Port-ankill and East Tarbit, called St. Medan's Cave; together with a pool in the adjoining rock, styled the well of the Co or the Chapel well—for this place often goes by the name of the Chapel. To bathe in this well as the sun rose, on the first Sunday in May, was considered an infallible cure for all manner of sickness. And till no very remote period, it was customary for almost the whole population of the parish, to collect at this spot on the first Sunday in May which was called Co Sunday, to bathe in the well, to leave their offerings in the cave, and to spend the day in gossiping or amusement.

SINGULAR OBITUARY ANNOUNCEMENT.

At the funerals of poor people in the parish of Borrowstouness or Bo'ness, the following strange custom has been frequently observed. The beadle promenades the streets with a bell, and intimates the death of the recent defunct, in this language: "All brethren and sisters, I let you to wit there is a brother (or sister) departed at the pleasure of the Almighty (here he lifted his hat). All those that come to the burial, come at — o'clock. The corpse is at —." He also walked before the corpse ringing his bell.

HOLY WELL OBSERVANCES IN KINCARDINESHIRE.

At Balmanno in the parish of Marykirk, Kincardineshire, there is a well called St. John's well, which was formerly regarded with great veneration. Mothers brought their children to be bathed in its waters. To show their gratitude to the Saint and in the hope that he would continue his patronage of the well, they put presents into the water, such as needles, pins, and shreds of their garments.

ANCIENT RACES AT KILMARNOCK.

The observances of Fastern's E'en were continued at Kilmarnock until of late years. These principally consisted of races, which were considered to be of great antiquity, having been practised annually for the last five centuries.

CREELING THE BRIDEGROOM AGAIN.

The ancient custom of creeling has already been pretty fully described but the following account of the ceremony as observed at Dalry will be interesting as the custom in some respects varied at different places. In former days when penny weddings were in vogue, it was customary for the parties who were at the wedding to assemble the following day in order to creel the bridegroom. Having procured a creel or wicker basket they tied it on the back of the young gude-man, and placed a long pole with a broom affixed to the top over his left shoulder. Thus equipped he was forced to run a race followed by the gudewife with a knife to cut the cords, and who according to the alacrity with which she strove to unloose the creel showed her satisfaction at the marriage; after which the parties returned to the house to consume the fragments of the preceding day's feast. About a century ago, weddings having become less numerously attended than formerly the custom underwent considerable alterations, and was deferred to New Year's day. Accordingly on this morning, the young men of the village assembled provided with a wicker hamper or crockery crate, filled with stones with which they visited the houses of all those who had entered the bonds of matrimony during the preceding year, and compelled each young gudeman to bear the creel to his nearest neighbour who might have qualified himself for this honour. Resistance was genally useless, as a number of stout fellows soon compelled the refractory party to submit with the addition probably of one of their number in the creel, as the reward of his obstinacy. The creeling however was generally conducted throughout with the greatest good humour, yet harmless as the custom was, individuals have been known, who in order to avoid the ceremony, absented themselves regularly for fifteen years from home, for a fortnight at that season.

OLD BORDER CUSTOMS.

Alarm signals were in use along the Borders and throughout Galloway. That no shire might want advertisement, it was thought proper that beacons should be set up on all heights of eminence within sight of each other, in order that the appearance of the enemy on the Borders or on the sea might be made known. A beacon was formed of a tall and strong tree set up with a long iron plate across its head, carrying on it an iron plate for holding a fire, and an iron brander fixed on a stalk in the middle for holding a tar barrel. The first fire was put on the ground beside the beacon, at sight whereof all were to fly to arms. The next advertisement was by two fires, the one on the ground and the other in the large grate. On seeing this, all were to hasten to the rendezvous. If the danger was imminent, to the two fires were added that of the burning barrel. Signals from Berwick up the vale of the Tweed to Lamberton, and from the Tweed to the Forth, made the whole country aware of the coming danger.

ALARM SIGNALS.

A fiery peat was sent round by the Borderers to alarm in times of danger, as the fiery cross was by the Highlanders.

LEAVING THE RIGHT HAND UNBAPTISED.

In the Border counties it was formerly the custom, to some extent, to leave the right hand of the male children un-baptised that it might deal more deadly, or according to the popular phrase, un-hallowed blows on their enemies.

GOOD FAITH OF THE BORDERERS.

As some atonement for their laxity of morals, on most occasions the Borderers were severe observers of the faith which they had pledged, even to an enemy. If any person broke his word so plighted, the individual to whom faith had not been observed, used to bring to the next Border meeting a glove hung on the point of a spear, and proclaim to Scots and English the name of the offender. This was accounted so great a disgrace to all connected with him, that his own clansmen sometimes destroyed him to escape the infamy he had brought upon them.

SUNDAY DISSIPATION.

Of the many customs at one time prevalent in Scotland, not a few have been altogether discontinued, others again are slowly but surely dying out. Among the former may be mentioned Sunday Sprees. These were long in high favour and were carried out to great lengths. Sabbath after Sabbath bands of disorderly men would meet in some appointed place, when drinking to great excess was indulged in. The proceedings commenced early in the morning, indeed they were generally the continuation of Saturday night's spree, and were not brought to a close until late on Sunday evening. It is said also that while the men held their orgies in t' e open air, the wives had their sprees within doors so that Sabbath desecration was the rule with both sexes. The Forbes Mackenzie Act however put a stop in a great measure to this Sunday debauchery, and though it was severely anathematised by the men at the time, the women hailed it as an unmixed blessing.

PUNISHMENT OF MATRIMONIAL INFIDELITY.

In old lawless times, one would be inclined to suppose that every sort of immorality would be condoned or at least overlooked. But it was not so. A man might indeed steal a sheep from among a flock passing through the village and be praised for his dexterity. He might slay his fellow in fair combat and be hailed as a hero. He might bear off the lass of his choice without the consent of her parents and be admired for his courage; but, if he fell in love with his neighbour's wife he had to run the gauntlet, and this assuredly was no child's play. At a stated time the villagers assembled in the aggressor's house, and stripping him to his shirt they tied him to the back of a pony cart which stood in readiness, his cast-off clothes being previously bundled up and thrown into it. In this manner he was made to march or run through the town followed by a hooting crowd who belaboured him as he went along. This continued till the procession reached the head of the village, when the fellow's hands were unloosed, his clothes flung at him, and he allowed to return or depart as he chose.

If on the other hand the culprit was a female her case was brought before a jury of matrons, and if found guilty she was subjected to the humiliating ordeal of riding the stang. Placed accordingly astride upon a pole or stang, the woman was hoisted on the shoulders of a number of men, and was carried high in the procession through the town amid the huzzas of the populace till arriving at some water, she was straightway tumbled in without further ceremony.

MARRIAGE PROCESSIONS.

Of customs which are dying out among us we may notice marriage processions. Not so very long ago, it used to be a regular practice in the parish for wedding parties to walk in procession, preceded by the fiddler, to the manse, there to take the vows of matrimony upon them, and returning not only themselves rejoicing but making the whole village to rejoice with them. These processions were much relished by the people.

ODD FOOTBALL CUSTOM.

The inhabitants of Foulden celebrated Fasten's E'en with a game of football. The villagers were arrayed against the inhabitants of the country; a large ball was thrown up into the air midway between the parish church and the mill. The former strove to lodge the ball in the church *pulpit*, and the latter in the mill *happer*.

SINGULAR HOLY WELL SUPERSTITION.

There is a loch in Strathnaver in Sutherland, to which people constantly resorted for all manner of cures. They must walk backwards into the water, take their dip, and leave a small coin as due offering. Then without looking round, they must walk straight back to the land, and so, right away from the loch.

St. Andrew's well in the Island of Lewis was frequently consulted as an oracle when any one was dangerously ill. A wooden tub full of this water was brought to the sick man's room, and a small dish was set floating on the surface of the water; if it turned sunwise it was supposed the patient would recover, otherwise he must die.

CURIOUS FISHING CUSTOM.

Superstitions which used to prevail among the villagers of Cockenzie, as in other fishing localities is now, owing to the better education of the people, happily dying out, but it is a well known fact that only a few years ago, no fisherman would have ventured out to sea had either a pig or a lame man crossed his path when on his way to the beach. Not only so, but had a stranger met him and been the first to greet him of a morning, with a *gude mornin*, he would have regarded the interruption as an evil omen, and remained at home for that day at least.

Another very curious and superstitious custom used to prevail among fisher people. If, when at sea, especially going out or coming into port, any one was heard to take the name of God in vain, the first to hear the expression immediately called out "cauld airn," when each of the boat's crew would instantly grasp fast the first piece of iron which came within his reach, and hold it for a time between his hands. This was by way of counteracting his ill luck, which otherwise would have continued to follow the boat for the remainder of the day.

THE SILLER GUN AT KIRKCUDBRIGHT.

The burgh of Kirkcudbright, like its neighbour Dumfries, is in possession of a silver gun which according to tradition was presented by King James VI. to the incorporated trades, to be shot for occasionally, in order that they might improve themselves in the use of firearms, then rapidly supplanting the bow and arrows as implements of war. The year 1587 is graven on the barrel of this miniature gun, and also the letters T. M. C., supposed to be the initials of Thomas M'Callum, of Bombie, ancestor of the Lords of Kirkcudbright, who was at that time Alderman of the burgh. This trinket, which greatly resembles a penny whistle, has only been shot for three times in the memory of that oft quoted individual, the oldest inhabitant's father. In the summer of 1781, the incorporated trades applied by petition to the magistrates to have the gun placed in the hands of their convener, that they might shoot for it at a target as formerly, which petition was granted. The next time it was shot for was on the 22nd of April, 1830, the day on which Lord Selkirk attained his majority. On this occasion the great wassail bowl of the burgh, which had been presented by Hamilton of Bargerry, M.P., was used for the first time since the Union. It was placed at the market cross, and after the gun had been contended for, the bowl was filled and refilled with potent liquor. The last time this gun was shot for was on the occasion of the Queen's coronation, on the 28th of June, 1838. After the match the bowl was filled at the expense of the town, and her Majesty's health drunk with the utmost enthusiasm. This capacious bowl is made of walnut hooped with brass, and is large enough to hold ten gallons.

CHAPTER XII.

Old Lammastide customs at Mid-Lothian—Some Galloway customs—Throwing the hoshen—Fykes Fair—Giving up the names—Old games—The priest's cat—Customs at new moon—Old marriage ceremonies—Bar for bar—The game of Blinchamps—The game of Burly Whush—The game of king and queen of Cantalon.

LAMMASTIDE CUSTOMS AT MID-LOTHIAN.

IN the first volume of the "Archæologia Scotica," published by the Society of Antiquaries of Scotland in 1792, there is a very good description of the manner in which the Lammas festival used to be celebrated in Mid-Lothian about the middle of the eighteenth century. From this paper it appears that all the herds within a certain district towards the beginning of summer associated themselves into bands, sometimes to the number of a hundred or more. Each of these communities agreed to build a tower in some conspicuous place near the centre of their district. This tower was usually built of sods, though sometimes of stones. It was for the most part square, about 4 feet in diameter at the bottom, and tapering to a point at the top, which was seldom above 7 feet or eight feet from the ground. In building it a hole was left in the centre for admitting a flagstaff, on which were displayed their colours on the great day of the festival. This tower was generally commenced about a month before Lammas, being seldom entirely completed till close upon that time. From the moment the foundation of the tower was laid it became an object of care and attention to the whole community, for it was reckoned a disgrace to suffer it to be defaced. As the honour that was acquired by the demolition of a tower, if effected by those belonging to another, was in proportion to the disgrace of suffering it to be demolished, each party endeavoured to circumvent the other as much as possible. To give the alarm of the approach of an attacking party, every person was armed with a tooting-horn. As the great day of Lammas approached, each community chose one from among themselves for their captain. They marched forth early in the morning on Lammas Day dressed in their best apparel, each armed with a stout cudgel, and, repairing to their tower, there displayed their colours in triumph. If news was brought that a hostile party approached, the horns sounded to arms. Seldom did they admit the approach of the enemy, but usually went forth to meet them. When the two parties met they mutually desired each other to lower their colours in sign of subjection, and if there appeared to be a great disproportion in the strength of the parties, the weakest usually submitted to this ceremony without much difficulty. But if they were nearly equal in strength none of them would yield, and the meeting ended in blows, and sometimes in bloodshed. When they had remained at their tower till about mid-day, if no opponent appeared, or if they themselves had no intention of making an attack, they then took down their colours and marched with horns sounding towards the most considerable village in their district, when the lasses and all the people came out to meet them and partake of their diversions. Boundaries were immediately appointed, and a proclamation made that all who intended to compete in the race should appear. A bonnet ornamented with ribbons was displayed upon a pole as the prize of the victor. The prize of the second race was a pair of garters, and the third a knife. When two parties met and one yielded to the other, they marched together for some time in two separate bodies, the subjected body behind the other; and then they parted good friends, each party performing their races at their own appointed place.

THE CUSTOM OF THROWING THE HOSHEN.

On the borders of Galloway when a young woman got married before her elder sister, this sister danced at her bridal without shoes. It was also customary here for the bride to remove her left stocking and throw it at random amongst the crowd. Whoever happened to catch it was the first to get married.

OLD FAIR CUSTOM IN GALLOWAY.

There was a singular fair called Fykes Fair held annually at the Clachan o' Auchencairn.

It began at *ten o'clock at night*, continuing till morning and through part of the next day. All the idle and dissolute characters in Galloway congregated in crowds at this fair.

CUSTOM REGARDING MARRIAGE ANNOUNCEMENT.

"Giving up the Names," is the designation of what used to be the ceremony attending the giving in to the precentor, the names of those intending to marry, to be proclaimed in church during Divine worship, so that any persons who wished to prevent such and such marriages from taking place might have an opportunity of stating their objections. They had the power of throwing down sixpence and protesting against such proceedings going any further. This was, however, seldom done. These names were generally given in on a Saturday night. In doing so the parties met in a public house. No females were present. The father or brother of the bride was her representative. The bridegroom and the best man were present. On the precentor being called in to attend the meeting the names were written down on a slip of paper, the bride's name by her male relation, and the bridegroom's by his best man. After this was done, whisky was introduced, and those present speedily became intoxicated.

OLD FIRESIDE GAMES.

There is a fireside game called the Priest's Cat. A piece of stick is made red in the fire; one hands it to another, saying—

> "About wi' that, about wi' that,
> Keep alive the Priest's Cat."

round goes the stick, and the person in whose hand the flame goes out has lost the wager, and must pay a forfeit. In olden times when the priest's cat died, great lamentation ensued throughout the country, as it was supposed to become transformed into some supernatural being or witch who might work mischief; so to keep it alive was a great matter.

There is another old and favourite fireside game played by youths and maidens amongst the peasantry, called Hey Willie Wine, and how Willie Wine. One of the latter addresses one of the former thus,—

> "Hey Willie wine, and how Willie wine,
> I hope for home you'll not incline;
> You had better stop and stay all night
> And I'll gie thee a lady bright."

Then he answers—

> "What will ye gie if I with thee bide
> To be my bonny blooming bride?"

Again she—

> "I'll gie ye, Kate o' Dinglebell,
> A bonny body like yoursell."

Then he—

> "I'll stick her up in the pear tree,
> I lo'ed her once, but she's no for me,
> Yet I thank you for your courtesy."

This game concludes with the girl proposing a maiden agreeable to the youth. Before the questions are put, the lad whispers to a companion the name he will stop with, so this one must be given before the dialogue ends. The chief aim of this somewhat whimsical amusement seems to be, to discover one another's sweethearts. In olden times these discoveries were considered very valuable.

The maidens in Galloway, in former days, when first they saw the new moon, sallied out of doors, and pulled a handful of grass, saying—

> "New moon, new moon, tell me if you can
> Gif I have a hair like the hair o' my gudeman?"

The grass was then brought into the house and carefully searched, and if a hair was found amongst it, which was not unfrequently the case, the colour of the hair determined that of the future husband. It was also an old custom, on first seeing the new moon, to turn money in the pocket.

BAR FOR BAR.

The Gallowegians are or were so fond of rhyme that they have a game connected with it. One of the players invents a rhyme, the next who follows must make one to rhyme with it, and at the same time agree with it in sense. The third follows and so on. Those who can invent the best and most rhymes wins the game, and are declared to have the most poetry in their composition.

OLD RUSTIC GAME.

There is a very curious rustic game termed Blinchamp. When a bird's nest is found, such as a *Corbie's*, or *Hoodiecrow's*, or that of any other bird that people dislike, the eggs are taken out of it and laid in a row a little way apart from each other. One of the players has then something bound over his eyes to prevent him from seeing. A stick is then put in his hand, and he walks forward, as he fancies straight up to the eggs, and strikes at them. Another succeeds him until they thus blind-folded break them all. Hence the term Blinchamp.

GAME OF BURLY WHUSH.

Burly Whush is the name given to a game played with the ball. The ball is thrown up on a house or wall by one of the players, who cries out the instant it is thrown to another to catch it before it falls to the ground. Then they all run off, excepting the one individual called, to a little distance, and if he fails to catch it, he calls out *burly whush*. Then the others are arrested in their flight, and must run no farther. He then singles out one of them, and throws the ball at him. He in his turn throws the ball, and so on. Should a house be near at hand, as is generally the case, and any of the party take refuge behind it, they must still show one of their hands past the corner to the *burly whush* man, who sometimes hits it with such force as to make it tingle for hours afterwards.

KING AND QUEEN OF CANTELON.

This used to be a favourite game with the Galloway youths. Two of the swiftest of them are placed between two *doons* or places of safety, situated about two hundred paces distant from each other. The other boys stand in one of these *doons*. Then two fleet youths come forward and address them with this rhyme—

> "King and Queen o' Cantelon
> How many miles to Babylon,
> Six or seven or a long eight?
> Try to win there wi' candle light."

Then out they all ran in hopes to get to Babylon or the other *doon* without being caught. Those captured ere they reach Babylon are not allowed to run again until all the others are taken, when a fresh game commences. This is a game of great antiquity, and is believed to be a mimic representation of scenes and characters in the time of the Crusades. The King and Queen of Cantelon are supposed to be King and Queen of Caledon, then the name Babylon, introduced into the rhyme, the long way they had to wander and the chance there was of their being caught by the infidels, all point to the origin of the game.

OLD MARRIAGE CEREMONIES.

Marriage ceremonies are not nearly of so much importance nor so well attended as formerly. Old women have been heard to say that the *spirit o' waddings* has left the country. *Waddin bawes*,—money tossed amongst the people at marriages. *Waddin braws,*—dresses for marriage. The buying of these braws was deemed a very serious affair, as it was the first time the young people appeared in public. *Waddin sarks*—the bride previous to marriage, in proof of her skill as a needlewoman, made the bridegroom a shirt,—hence the above term. A peasant once remarked to a friend, "that he really never intended to take Maggie (his wife), but the cutty saw this, flew to his neck, and measured him for *the* sark, and so he was obliged to have her."

CHAPTER XIII.

Superstitious customs with regard to good or bad omens— Yule boys—The rumbling well in Galloway —Marrying days in Galloway—Michaelmas custom in Argyleshire—Saint Cowie and Saint Couslan— The lucky well of Beothaig—The bridge of one hair in Kincardineshire—The old custom of Rig and Rennel—Some old customs of the Sinclairs.

SUPERSTITIOUS CUSTOMS REGARDING GOOD OR BAD OMENS.

THERE used to be numerous superstitious observances with respect to good or bad omens, such as the shoes being twisted off the hoofs of asses before they had foals. A horseshoe passed thrice beneath the stomach and over the back of a cow supposed to have the elfshot (a disease with cows), then elfsgirse (a kind of grass given to cows believed to be injured by the elves) given to this cow, and a burning peat laid down on the threshold of the byredoor, she is set free from her stake and driven out. If she walks quietly over the peat she remains uncured; but if she first smells, then springs over it, she is cured. If, at a funeral, one of the handspoke-bearers turned his foot and fell beneath the bier, he would soon be in a coffin himself. If on the way to execute an errand but had forgot something, we should have no luck that day. Should a hare have crossed our path that was a bad omen. If a knife was found lying open on the ground few would dare to lift it. Even a pin, should the point be turned towards oneself, would not be touched. A broom was thrown after curlers when they left a house, for good luck. There was also an omen of the *blue dead lights* which were supposed to be seen before death, these lights were seen in the air about the height at which a corpse was carried. If seen to leave the house where the person was to die, and go to the spot in the churchyard where he should be buried, to stop these lights was thought very improper.

The first three days of April are called "borrowing days," and the *freets* regarding them run so—

> "March borrows frae April,
> Three days and they are ill.
> The first of them is wind and weet,
> The second it is snow and sleet,
> The third of them is peel-a-bane
> And freezes the wee birds nebs tae the stane."

Magpies caused other curious *freets*, according to the number of them seen at one time together.

> "Ane's sorrow, two's mirth,
> Three's a burial, four's a birth.
> Five's a wedding, six brings scaith,
> Seven's money, eight's death."

A mist about the last day of the moon's decline always brought with it a *freet*—

> "An auld moon's mist
> Never dies o' thirst."

It is said of February—

> "February fills the dyke
> Either wi' black or white."

And of Candlemas day—

> If Candlemas day be fair and clear
> We'll have two winters in that year.

And gin the laverock (lark) sings before Candlemas she'll mourn as long after it.

YULE BOYS.

Boys who rambled through the country during the Christmas holidays were called Yule Boys. They were all dressed in white save one, the Beelzebub of the party. They had a singular rhyme which they repeated before the people, and so received money and cake. This rhyme is now so sadly shorn of its original proportions that its real meaning can scarcely be arrived at. It evidently, however, is of ancient origin. In old Scottish books some notice is taken of the *quhite boys of Yule*. The plot of the doggerel seems to be that two knights dispute about a lady and fight. One of them falls and sings out—

> "A doctor! a doctor! or I die."

Beelzebub sings—

> "A doctor, doctor, here am I."

The wounded knight sayeth,

> "What can you cure?"

Beelzebub answereth—

> "All disorders to be sure,
> From the cramp to the gout.
> Cut off legs and arms,
> Join them to again," etc. etc.

THE RUMBLING WELL IN GALLOWAY.

In the parish of Bootle, Galloway, is a well called the Rumbling well, which was formerly frequented by crowds of sick people on the first Sunday in May. They lay by its side all Saturday night and drank of it early in the morning. There is also another well about a quarter of a mile distant towards the east. This well was made use of by the people when their cattle were attacked by a disease called *Connach*. This water they came from distant parts to obtain. They carried it away in vessels, washed their cows in it, and then gave it them to drink. At both wells they left thank-offerings, money at the former, and at the latter the bands and shackles wherewith beasts are usually bound.

MARRYING DAYS IN GALLOWAY.

Marriages in Galloway in olden times were commonly celebrated on Tuesdays and Thursdays. The Rev. Dr. Simpson, of Sanquhar, asserted that out of 450 marriages which he himself celebrated, all, except seven, took place on these days.

MICHAELMAS CUSTOM IN ARGYLESHIRE.

The following singular custom at one time existed at Canway, Argyllshire. On Michaelmas day every man mounted his horse, unfurnished with saddle, and took behind him either some young girl or his neighbour's wife, and they rode backwards and forwards from the village to a certain cross, without any of them being able to account for the origin of this custom. After the procession was over, they alighted at some public-house, where, strange to say, the females entertained the companions of their ride. After their return to their houses an entertainment of primeval simplicity was prepared. The chief part consisted of a great oat-cake called *Struan Michael*, or St. Michael's Cake, composed of two pecks of meal, and formed like the quadrant of a circle. It was daubed over with milk and eggs, and then placed to harden before the fire.

ST. COWIE AND ST. COUSLAN.

The parish of Campbeltown formerly consisted of four distinct parishes, two of which were respectively dedicated to St. Cowie and

St. Couslan. These two saints, who were pious, holy men, and who wrought equally for the improvement of their respective parishes, held, it would seem, very different ideas in respect to marriage. Couslan, for instance, inculcated in the strongest manner the indissolubility of the marriage tie; and if lovers did not find it convenient to go through the marriage ceremony, their joining hands through a hole in a small pillar near his church was held an interim tie of mutual fidelity so strong and sacred that it was firmly believed in the country that no man ever broke it who did not soon after break his neck or meet with some other fatal accident.

Cowie, in his district, took quite a different course. He proposed that all who did not find themselves happy and contented in the married state should be indulged with an opportunity of parting and making a second choice. For that purpose he instituted an annual solemnity, at which all the unhappy couples in his parish were to assemble at his church ; and at midnight all present were blindfolded and ordered to run round the church at full speed, with a view of *mixing the lots in the urn.* The moment the ceremony was over, without allowing an instant for the people present to recover from their confusion, the word *cabbay* (seize quickly) was pronounced, upon which every man laid hold of the first female he met with. Whether old or young, handsome or ugly, good or bad, she was his wife till the next anniversary of this strange custom, when an opportunity was afforded him of getting a worse or a better bargain. In this way the Saint soon brought his parishioners to understand that they had reason to be satisfied with a condition there was little prospect of mending by a change. This tradition has been handed down for centuries.

THE LUCKY WELL OF BEOTHAIG.

There is a well in the parish of Gigha, in Argyllshire, called *Tabarreth Blueathaig, i.e.,* the Lucky Well of Beothaig, a well famous for having the command of the wind. It is situated at the foot of a hill fronting the north-east, near an isthmus called Tarbet. Six feet above where the water gushes out there is a heap of stones which forms a cover to the sacred fount. When a person wished for a fair wind, either to leave the land or to bring home his absent friends, this part was opened with great solemnity, the stones carefully removed, and the well cleaned out with a wooden dish or clam shell. This being done, the water was thrown several times in the direction from which the wished-for wind was to blow. This action was accompanied by a certain form of words which the person repeated every time he threw the water. When the ceremony was finished, the well was again carefully covered up to prevent fatal consequences, it being firmly believed that were the place left open a storm would inevitably destroy the entire locality.

THE BRIDGE OF ONE HAIR.

In the month of May numbers of the working classes came from the adjacent districts to drink out of a well in the Bay of Nigg, Kincardineshire, called Douny well, and proceeding a little further, they went across a narrow pass called the *Brig o' ae Hair*—the bridge of one hair—to Douny Hill, a green island in the sea, where young people carved their favourite names in the sward. This custom seemed to be the remains of some superstitious respect to the fountain and retreat of a favourite saint. The bay, probably from the corruption of his name, was formerly called St. Fittick's Bay. On the sudden deaths of their relations, or when in fear of such catastrophe from the sea becoming stormy, the fisher people, especially the females, expressed their sorrow by exclamations of voice and gestures of body like the eastern nations.

THE CUSTOM OF RIG AND RENNEL.

The somewhat peculiar custom of Rig and Rennel, or run rig, *i.e.*, that each tenant on a particular farm or district had a ridge alternately with his neighbour, formerly prevailed over the north, and lingered in Caithness till 1740. This arrangement naturally caused confusion and disputes. It is believed to have been instituted in barbarous times as a preservative against one neighbour setting fire to the field of another if on bad terms with him, and to make them all equally anxious to resist the foe in case of invasion.

SOME SINGULAR OLD CUSTOMS.

All gentlemen of the name of Sinclair belonging to Conisbury, used carefully to avoid putting on green attire or crossing the Ord upon a Monday. They were dressed in green and they crossed the Ord upon a Monday when they marched to Flodden, where they fought and fell. On this account both the day and the dress were deemed unlucky. If the Ord had to be got over on a Monday the journey was performed by sea.

CHAPTER XIV.

Some old customs at Wick—Funeral processions at North Uist—Marriage customs among the poorer classes in the North—Going a rocking—Old customs in the Orkney Islands—Fishermen's customs in setting out for the fishing ground—The sow's day—St. Peter's day—Dingwall Court of Justice—Old custom at Eriska—Singular fisherman's custom at Fladda—Interesting Highland custom—Old customs at the Island of Eigg.

SOME OLD CUSTOMS AT WICK.

IT was recently a custom for people to visit the Chapel of St. Tears, Wick, dedicated to the Holy Innocents, on St. Innocent's day, and leave in it bread and cheese as an offering to the souls of the children slain by Herod. Till within a few years ago, the inhabitants of Mirelandorn used to visit the Kirk of Moss every Christmas before sunrise, placing on a stone bread and cheese, and a silver coin, which, as they alleged, disappeared in some mysterious manner. There are still several holy lochs, especially one at Dunnet, to which people go from Wick, and indeed from all parts of Caithness, to be cured of their diseases. They cast a penny into the water, walk or are carried round the loch and return home. If they recover, their cure is ascribed to the mystic virtues of the *Hulie* Loch; and if they do not, their want of faith gets all the blame.

FUNERAL PROCESSIONS AT NORTH UIST.

The former inhabitants of North Uist used to conduct their funerals with remarkable solemnity. The coffin was followed by pipers playing slow plaintive dirges, composed for, and only played on these occasions. On arriving near the churchyard the music ceased, and the procession formed a line on either side, between which the corpse was carried to the grave.

MARRIAGE CUSTOMS AMONG THE POOR IN THE NORTH.

Marriages amongst the poorer classes of the North were somewhat similar to penny weddings. The relatives who assembled in the morning were regaled with a glass of whiskey *gratis*, but after the ceremony every man paid for what he drank. The neighbours then assembled in great numbers, and danced to the lively strains of a couple of fiddles, at intervals, for two or three days. The merrymaking ended with Saturday night. On Sunday, after returning from church, the newly-married couple gave a dinner to their relations on both sides.

THE OLD CUSTOM OF GOING A ROCKING.

It was formerly customary in the West of Scotland for women, when invited to a social meeting at a neighbour's house, to take with them *rocks*, or distaffs, which, being very portable, proved no incumbrance to them on these occasions. Hence the phrase of *going a rocking*. Burns commences one of his songs with an allusion to this custom—

"On Fasten's e'en (Shrove Tuesday) we had a rocking."

OLD CUSTOMS IN THE ORKNEY ISLANDS.

Owing to the long residence of the Bishops amongst the inhabitants of the Orkney Islands both before and after the Reformation; as well as the splendid external show in the Episcopal form of worship, such a deep impression was produced by Episcopacy on the minds of the people that it has not yet yielded to the lapse of time. To many of the old places of worship, especially those dedicated to favourite saints, they attached great veneration, visiting them frequently when in a serious, melancholy, or devout frame of mind. Within their ruined walls they used to repeat prayers and use forms of words, of whose meaning they were entirely ignorant; and when they considered themselves threatened by any danger they invoked the aid of their saints, and vowed to perform services or present oblations to them on condition that they interfered successfully in their behalf. If they imagined the saint invoked, had interfered to prevent the threatened calamity they were for the greater part very punctual in performing their vows. Some days on which to commence important business were esteemed by them lucky, others were deemed equally unlucky. Some months, in their estimation, were preferable to others. Thursdays and Fridays were the days on which they liked to marry. They scrupulously avoided marriage when the moon was on the wane. If they killed cattle they did so when it was on the increase, from an idea that should they delay doing so until the moon was waning the meat would be of an inferior description. In preparing for a voyage, when leaving the shore they always turned their boats in the direction of the sun's course; in some places they never omitted offering up a prayer on these occasions.

The festivals in the Romish Calendar were scrupulously observed in these islands, not, however, as days of religious worship, but as holidays to be devoted to feasting and merry-making. On some of these days they chose to remain entirely idle. On others they engaged in particular kinds of work. Now they ate flesh and meat; again, eggs and milk. They possessed innumerable charms for killing sparrows, which eat the early corn, and for securing a successful brewing of ale, and the churning of milk, as well as those which brought good luck, cured the toothache, rheumatism, &c.

Before striking their tents at Lammas and bidding farewell for a while to the active perilous occupations of the summer, the Orkney fishermen who had been accustomed to associate during the season met and partook of a parting cup, when the usual toast was, "Lord, open Thou the mouth of the grey fish and hold Thy hand above the corn." This meeting was known by the name of the Fishers' Foy.

In one part of the parish of Sandwick, in Orkney, every family that owned a herd of swine killed a sow on the 17th of December. This day, in consequence, was called Sow's Day. No tradition is handed down to account for the origin of this custom. The people of Sandwick also did no work on the 3rd of March, in commemoration of the day on which the church was consecrated. The church being dedicated to St. Peter, they all abstained from working for themselves on St. Peter's Day, but they would do any kind of labour for any other person who chose to employ them.

OLD CUSTOM AT DINGWALL.

The inhabitants of Dingwall formerly had a tradition among them to the effect that after a man had received sentence of death in the Court of Justice, formerly held in a house in this parish, he obtained remission of his sentence provided he made his escape through the crowd of people on the lake-side, and touched the steeple of the church before any one could lay hold on him.

OLD CHURCH CUSTOMS.

There is a stone set up about a mile to the south of St. Columba's Church, Eriska, about eight feet high, and two broad. It is called by the natives the Bowing Stone, for when the inhabitants first came in sight of the church, they set up this stone and there bowed and said the Lord's Prayer.

There is a church in Fladda dedicated to St. Columba. It has an altar in the east end, and there is a blue stone of a round form on it which is always moist. It was an ordinary custom when any of the fishermen were detained in the island by contrary winds to wash this blue stone with water, thereby expecting to procure a favourable breeze. This practice was said never to fail, especially if a stranger washed the stone.

INTERESTING OLD HIGHLAND CUSTOM.

It was formerly the custom in the Western Islands when any number of men retired to a house either to discuss matters of business, or to indulge in drinking, to allow the doors of the house to stand open, and to put a rod across the door. This was intended for a sign to people not to intrude upon their privacy.

OLD CUSTOM AT THE ISLAND OF EIGG.

In the village on the south coast of the island of Eigg, there is a well called St. Katherine's well. The natives have it in great esteem and believe it to be a Catholicon for diseases. According to Martin (1696) this well was consecrated by one Father Hugh, a Catholic priest, in the following manner. He obliged all the inhabitants to come to it and then employed them to bring together a great heap of stones at the head of the spring by way of penance. This being done, Father Hugh said mass at the well and then consecrated it. He also gave each of the inhabitants a piece of wax candle which they lighted, and all of them made the dessil of going round the well sunwise, the priest leading them, and from that time it has been accounted unlawful to boil any meat with the water of this well. The natives observe St. Katherine's anniversary after this fashion. They come to the well, and having drank a draught of it, they make the dessil round it sunwise, and then return home.

CHAPTER XV.

Interesting customs at St. Kilda—The water-cross at Barra—Ocean Meat—Curious wooing custom in the Western Islands—Annual Festival in honour of St. Barr—The fiery circle—Old customs in the Island of Lewis—Singular cure for Scrofula—Strange custom regarding forced fire—Devotion to St. Flannan—Salmon-fishing Superstition—The Sea-god Shoney—Burying custom at Taransay—Michaelmas custom at Lingay—Customs regarding fowling expeditions.

INTERESTING CUSTOMS AT ST. KILDA.

THE primitive inhabitants of the lonely island of St. Kilda formerly left off working at twelve o'clock on Saturday, as an ancient custom handed down from their fathers, and went no more to it again till Monday morning. They used a set form of prayers at the hoisting of their sails. They lay down at night, rose again in the morning, and began their labours always in the name of God. Upon the anniversary of All Saints, the inhabitants of St. Kilda had an annual cavalcade; the number of their horses never exceeded eighteen. These they mounted by turns, having neither saddle nor bridle of any kind except a rope, which managed the horse only on one side. They rode from the sea shore to their houses, and when each man had performed his turn the show was at an end. On this festival they baked a large cake in form of a triangle, but rounded, and it had to be all eaten that night. Their marriages were celebrated in the following manner. When any two of them had agreed to take one another for man and wife, the officer who presided over the island summoned all the inhabitants of both sexes to Christ's Chapel, where being assembled, he enquired publicly if there were any lawful impediment why these parties should not be joined in the bands of holy matrimony. If no objection was made to the proposed union, he then enquired of the parties if they were resolved to live together in weal and woe, etc. After their assent, he declared them married persons, and then desired them to ratify this solemn promise in the presence of God and the people. In order that they might do this, the Crucifix was tendered to them, and both put their right hands upon it, this being the ceremony by which lovers swore fidelity one to another during their life-time.

Their baptisms were formerly conducted in the following manner. The parents called in the officer or any one of their neighbours to baptise the child, and another to be sponsor. He who performed the office of clergyman, being told what the child's name was to be, said (naming it), "I baptise you to your father and your mother in the name of the Father, Son, and Holy Ghost." Then the sponsor took the child in his arms, as also did his wife as god-mother, and ever after this there was a friendship between the parents and the sponsor esteemed so sacred and inviolable, that nothing was able to set them at variance; and it reconciled those who had been at enmity previously.

There is a famous stone in St. Kilda, known as the Mistress Stone. It exactly resembles a door, and is in the front of a perpendicular rock twenty or thirty fathoms in height. Upon the lintel of this door, every bachelor-wooer was by an ancient custom obliged in honour to give the beloved one the following singular proof of his affection. He had to stand on his left foot, having the one half of it over the rock. He then drew his right foot towards the left, and, in this posture, bowing, put both his fists further out to the right foot. After he had performed this feat he acquired no small reputation, being even accounted worthy the finest woman in the world. It was firmly believed this achievement was always attended with the desired success.

Martin (1696) tells us that the Steward of St. Kilda was accustomed in time of a storm to tie a bundle of puddings made of the fat of sea-fowl to the end of his cable, and let it fall into the sea behind the rudder. This, he said, hindered the waves from breaking, and calmed the sea. The scent of the grease, however, attracted the whales, so says Martin, which put the vessel in danger.

OLD CUSTOM AT BARRA.

A stone in the form of a cross stood near to St. Mary's Church, in the Island of Barra. The natives called it the Water Cross, the ancient inhabitants having a custom of erecting it to procure rain, and, when procured, the cross was laid flat on the ground.

OCEAN MEAT AT KISMULL.

The inhabitants of the Island of Kismull had formerly a custom that when any strangers from the northern islands resorted thither, the natives, immediately after their landing, obliged them to eat, no matter how heartily they may have eaten before starting on their journey. This meal was styled Biey Tai, *i.e.*, Ocean Meat. Whatever number of strangers came there, or of whatever quality or sex, they were hospitably installed one each in a family. According to this custom, husbands and wives were forced to live apart while in this island.

CURIOUS WOOING CUSTOM IN THE WESTERN ISLANDS.

In the good old times, when a tenant's wife, in the Island of Linnell or the adjoining islands, died, he at once addressed himself to MacNeil of Barra, and begged him to provide him with another wife to manage his affairs. Upon this representation, MacNeil found out a suitable match for him; and, informed of the woman's name, he immediately went to her with a bottle of whisky, for their entertainment at their marriage, which at once took place. When a tenant died his widow in similar fashion was soon provided with another partner.

ANNUAL FESTIVAL OF ST. BARR.

All the inhabitants of Barra formerly

observed the anniversary of St. Barr, being the 27th of September. The ceremony was performed riding on horseback, and the solemnity was concluded by the cavalcade going three times round St. Barr's Church. They had likewise a grand procession on St. Michael's day in Killor village, where they also took a turn round the church. Every family, as soon as the solemnity was ended, were accustomed to bake St. Michael's cake, and all strangers, together with the members of the household, were obliged to eat the bread that night.

THE FIERY CIRCLE.

It was formerly the custom in the Island of Lewis to make a fiery circle about the houses, corn, cattle, etc., belonging to each particular family. A man carried fire in his right hand and went round. This practice was called *Dessil;* the right hand being in ancient language called dess. Another ancient custom observed in this Island by the Catholics on the second of February was this. The mistress and servants of each family took a sheaf of oats and dressed it in woman's apparel, put it in a large basket, and laid a wooden club by it; and this they called brüdes-bed. Then the mistress and servants shouted aloud, "Brüd is come—Brüd is welcome." This they did just before going to bed. In the morning when they rose they looked anxiously amongst the ashes expecting to see the impressions of Brüd's club there. If seen, it was reckoned a true presage of a good crop and a prosperous year.

OLD CUSTOMS IN THE ISLAND OF LEWIS.

In the Isle of Lewis it was customary for the seventh son to give a silver sixpence with a hole in it to each scrofulous patient. The coin was strung on a thread, and the sufferer wore it constantly round his neck. Should he lose it, the malady returned. Age was of no account in regard to this magic gift. The smallest child might heal the aged man. All that was requisite was, that some one should take the little hand and apply it to the sore. The belief was pretty general throughout the North-Western Highlands and Isles, that scrofula would certainly be cured by the touch of the seventh son of a woman, who had never a girl born between.

The inhabitants of Lewis formerly made use of a fire called *Tin-Egin*, a forced, or fire of necessity, which they used as an antidote against the plague, or murrain in cattle. It was prepared thus. All the fires in the parish were extinguished, and then, eighty-one married men, that being considered the necessary number, took two great planks of wood, and nine of them were employed alternately to rub one of the planks against the other until the heat thereof produced fire. From this forced fire each family was supplied with new fire, which was no sooner kindled than a pot of water was quickly placed on it. The people infected by the plague, and the latter suffering from the murrain, were afterwards sprinkled with water from the pot.

In Martin's tour (1696) in the Hebrides, it is stated that when the men of Lewis made expeditions to the rocky Island of St. Flannan in pursuit of sea fowl, as soon as they had effected the different landings they uncovered their heads and made a turn sunwise, thanking God for their safety. They then repaired to the little chapel of St. Flannan, on approaching which they advanced on their knees towards the chapel, and so went round the little building in procession. They then set to work, rock-fowling till the hour of vespers, when the same ceremony was repeated. They held it unlawful to kill any sea-bird after evening prayer, and in any case might never kill a bird with a stone. The contrary was regarded a bad omen.

The inhabitants of the village of Barva, Lewis, long retained an ancient custom of sending a man very early in the morning to cross Barvas river, every first day of May, in order to prevent any female from crossing it first. For that, they said, would prevent the salmon from coming into the river all the year round. This assertion they maintained to be true from experience.

THE SEA-GOD SHONEY.

The inhabitants in the vicinity of Siant had an ancient custom of sacrificing to a sea-god called Shoney, at Hallow-tide, in which the inhabitants of the neighbouring islands also took part. They assembled at the Church of Mulvay, having each man his provisions along with him. Every family furnished a peck of malt, and this was brewed into ale. One of the number was picked out to wade into the sea up to the middle, carrying a cup of ale in his hand. Standing in this posture he called out in a loud voice, saying, " Shoney, I give you this cup of ale hoping that you will be so kind as to send us plenty of sea-ware for enriching our ground this ensuing year." With these words the ale was thrown into the sea. This was done in the night time. On his returning those assembled all repaired to church where there was a candle burning upon the altar. After standing silent for a little while, one of them gave a signal upon which the candle was put out, and all adjourned to the fields, where they drank their ale, and spent the remainder of the night in dancing and singing.

OLD BURYING CUSTOM AT TARANSAY.

It was formerly the custom in the island of Taransay never to bury a man in St. Tarian's Chapel, or a woman in St. Keith's, otherwise the corpse, it was firmly believed, would be found above ground the day after its interment.

MICHAELMAS CUSTOM AT LINGAY.

The natives of the island of Lingay had an anniversary cavalcade on Michaelmas day, and then all ranks of both sexes appeared on horseback. The place of rendezvous was a large piece of fine sandy ground on the seashore, and there they had horse-racing, for small prizes, which were eagerly contended for. There was an ancient custom here by which it was lawful for any of the inhabitants to steal his neighbour's horse the night before the race, and ride it all that day provided he returned it safe and sound to the owner after the race. The manner of racing was rather curious. It was engaged in by a few young men who used neither saddles nor bridles, except two small ropes, nor any sort of spurs but their bare heels, and when they began the race they threw those ropes on the horses necks, and drove them vigorously with a long piece of sea-ware in each hand instead of a whip, which had been dried in the sun several months previously for that purpose. The men had their sweethearts behind them on horseback, and they gave and received mutual presents. The men presented the women with knives and purses, while the women gave the men pairs of garters of divers colours. They presented them also with a quantity of wild carrots.

FOWLING CUSTOMS AT THE ISLAND OF MORE.

The island of More bears the ruins of a Chapel dedicated to St. Flannan. When the inhabitants came within about twenty paces of the altar they stripped themselves of their upper garments and laid them upon a stone which stood there for that purpose. Those who intended setting out upon a fowling expedition prayed three times. The first day they said the first prayers, advancing towards the Chapel on their knees. Their second prayers were said as they went round the Chapel. The third were said close by or in the Chapel.

CHAPTER XVI.

Form of prayer used for blessing a ship in the Western Islands—Dedicating horses to the sun at Iona—Curious Harvest custom in Island of Skye—Drinking custom in the Clan Macleod—Old customs in connection with a Holy Loch in Skye—The Evil Eye in the Western Islands—Signalling customs in olden times—Evening amusements in the Western Islands in former times—Curious belief regarding Quarrelling and Herrings—Belief in Brownies in the Western Islands.

BLESSING A SHIP IN THE WESTERN ISLANDS.

IT was an ancient custom in the Western Islands to hang a he-goat to the boat's mast, the inhabitants hoping thereby to secure a favourable wind. Also in setting out on an expedition by sea the following form of Divine invocation was used :—

The Steerman says—
"Let us bless our ship."
The answer by all the crew—
"God the Father bless her."
Steersman—
"Let us bless our ship."
Answer—
"Jesus Christ bless her."
Steersman—
"Let us bless our ship."
Answer—
"The Holy Ghost bless her."
Steersman—
"What do you fear since God the Father is with you."
Answer—
"We do not fear anything."
Steersman—
"What do you fear since God the Son is with you?"
Answer—
"We do not fear anything."
Steersman—
"What do you fear since God the Holy Ghost is with you?"
Answer—
"We do not fear anything."

Steersman—

"God the Father Almighty, for the love of Jesus Christ his Son, by the comfort of the Holy Ghost, the one God, who marvellously brought the children of Israel through the red sea, and brought Jonah to land out of the whale's belly, and the Apostle St. Paul, and his ship safely through the treacherous raging sea, and from the violence of a tempestuous storm, bless and conduct us peaceably, calmly, and comfortably through the sea to our harbour, according to His Divine will, which we beg, saying, Our Father, etc."

DEDICATING HORSES TO THE SUN.

Even in the last century Pennant was told by Bishop Pocock that on the eve of St. Michael the islanders of Iona brought all their horses to a small green hill whereon stood a circle of stones surrounding a cairn. Round this hill they all made the turn sunwise, thus unwittingly dedicating their horses to the sun.

HARVEST CUSTOM IN SKYE.

The following custom prevailed in the Island of Skye during the course of last century. The farmer who had first finished his reaping, sent a man or a maiden, with a bundle of corn to his next neighbour, who had not yet reaped down his harvest. He, in his turn, when finished, sent a similar bundle to his neighbour, who was behind with his work, and so on until all the corn was cut down. This sheaf was called *an gaolbir bhaeagh*, and was intended to convey a rebuke to the farmer for being so slow in comparison with his neighbours. The person who took upon himself the task of leaving the *an gaolbir bhaeagh* at the house of the dilatory farmer, was obliged to make good his retreat in case of his being caught, otherwise he would have experienced a sound thrashing for his pains.

DRINKING CUSTOM IN THE CLAN MACLEOD.

At Dunvegan Castle, Island of Skye, is still preserved the large horn known as Rory More's horn. It holds rather more than a bottle and a half. Every Laird of Macleod was, it is said, obliged on his coming of age, in proof of his manhood, to drain it full of claret, without once laying it down.

OLD HOLY LOCH CUSTOMS IN THE ISLAND OF SKYE.

At a certain place in the parish of Kilmuir, Isle of Skye, an accidental conflux of pure fresh water springs from a small elliptical pond of considerable depth. The bottom consists of whitish sand which, by being visible through the transparent waters, gives a beautiful greenish tint to the whole. This small lake is surrounded by a little brushwood, and the rivulet which flows from it into the sea, is pleasantly hemmed in and edged with a few shrubs and bushes. This pond was anciently called Loch Sianta, which means the sacred lake, and it retains its name to this day. The hallowed appearance of the solitude did not escape the fancy of the ancient highlander. Owing to its crystalline purity and copiousness, and the sequestered situation of the little Hebridean Siloam, they conceived it to be favoured with its divinity, to whom they were extremely punctual in making offerings of various kinds. Invalids always resorted thither, and imagined themselves benefited by drinking of its water, and thoroughly washing themselves in a bath erected for the purpose. Pilgrimages are still made to Loch Sianta, and the usual turn sunwise must be made thrice before drinking.

THE EVIL EYE.

Among the superstitions of the people of the Western Islands, it may be noticed that there was nothing so much dreaded by many as what they termed the evil eye. As an antidote against this, the following verse was to be repeated in Gaelic by the person who dreaded it, when washing in the morning,—

"Let God bless my eye
And my eye will bless all I see;
I will bless my neighbours,
And my neighbours will bless me."

SIGNALLING CUSTOMS IN OLDEN TIMES.

On the west side of the parish of Strath are the ruins of seven Danish duns or forts. They are situated on high rocks or lofty headlands, and were built without mortar. One of these was always erected in view of one or more of the rest, so that the first alarm of an approaching foe was almost instantaneously communicated to the whole country by the *crois-taraidds*, or fiery cross, being a rude process of telegraphing by fire the intelligence of an enemy's approach. This watch-fire was lighted on the tower from which the danger was first perceived. The process was repeated by the neighbouring tower, and so on until the intelligence was transmitted with inconceivable celerity throughout the whole chain of towers with which the country was surrounded.

EVENING AMUSEMENTS IN THE WESTERN ISLANDS.

It was formerly the custom in the Western

Islands for neighbours to visit each other's houses almost nightly, and to while away part of the long winter evenings in reciting tales and traditions, singing songs, or playing some musical instrument. Now much of this is given up. The people have also abandoned their old customs when solemnizing funerals and marriages. Not very many years ago the memory of a person would have been thought dishonoured unless from fifty to sixty individuals accompanied his remains to the grave; and during the *farair*, or wake, and especially on the day of interment, such a quantity of meat and drink was distributed as kept the nearest surviving relatives for several years in the greatest poverty in order to pay for them. Then, again, such a quantity of whisky was drunk in the church or churchyard after the interment, that the people often forgot the solemnity of the occasion which had brought them together, and renewed former feuds and discussions, and fought fiercely amid the graves of their ancestors. A violent reaction, however, has taken place in the feelings and customs of the inhabitants in regard to the obsequies of their friends; and the change in regard to marriages is equally great. Formerly from eighty to a hundred persons used to assemble and pass at least two days in feasting and dancing. Now the guests are few in number, and the refreshments are generally restricted to herrings and potatoes. Balls and dancing parties have also been given up, and all public gatherings, whether for shinty, putting the stone, music, or dancing.

CURIOUS BELIEF REGARDING HERRINGS.

It was formerly asserted that if a quarrel happened on the coast where herrings were caught, and blood was shed, the herrings went away and never returned throughout that season.

Some time ago the natives of some of the Western Islands firmly believed in the existence of the gruagach, a female spectre of the class of brownies to whom the dairymaids made frequent libations of milk. The gruagach was said to be an innocent being who frolicked or gambolled among the pens and folds. She was armed solely with a pliable rod, with which she switched any who would annoy her either by using bad language, or by depriving her of her share of the dairy produce. Even so late as 1770, the dairymaids who attended a herd of cattle in the Island of Trodda, were in the habit of placing daily a quantity of milk on a hollow stone for the gruagach. Should they ever neglect this duty, they were sure to feel the weight of the brownie's rod on the day following.

CHAPTER XVII.

Some interesting customs and superstitions in Shetland—Observance of Yule-tide—Strange funeral custom—The water of health—The healing thread—Curing ringworm—Curing burns—Elf-shot—Wearing charms—Singular calving custom—Belief in fairies—The doings of fairies—The high land of the trows—Superstition regarding neighbour's profits—The neagle—Casting the heart.

INTERESTING OLD CUSTOMS IN SHETLAND.

THE ancient customs of guising or masquerading—a pastime peculiar to the observance of Yule-tide in Shetland—is still kept up with some of its accustomed spirit. The streets of Lerwick during the morning, to some extent, present the appearance of a Continental town during a carnival.

In some parts of Shetland, on a funeral procession passing, the by-standers used to throw three clods, one by one, after the corpse.

There is a spring in Unst called Yelaburn, or Hielaburn, the water of health. It was customary in former times, on first approaching the well, to throw three stones towards it as a tribute to the source of these salubrious waters. But its reputation has declined with the flight of time, and the superstitious offering is no longer religiously paid.

THE HEALING THREAD.

In these parts, in former times, when a person received a sprain, it was customary for him to apply to an individual practised in casting the wresting thread. This is a thread spun from black wool on which are cast nine knots. Tying it round the affected limb, the wise man said, but in a low tone of voice, so as not to be heard by the by-standers nor by the person operated upon—

"The Lord rade
And the foal slade;
He lighted
And He righted.

> Let joint to joint,
> Bone to bone,
> And sinew to sinew,
> Heal in the Holy Ghost's name."

FUNERAL CUSTOM.

It was a custom with some to burn the straw on which a dead body had lain, and to examine the ashes narrowly, from the belief that the print of the individual's foot who was next to be carried to the grave would be discovered. The straw was set on fire when the body was lifted and the funeral company leaving the house.

CURING RINGWORM.

The person afflicted with ringworm takes a few ashes, held between the forefinger and thumb, three successive mornings before tasting food, and, applying the ashes to the part afflicted, says—

> " Ringworm ! ringworm red !
> Never mayest thou either speed or spread ;
> But aye grow less and less,
> And die away among the ase (ashes)."

At the same time he throws the ashes, held between the finger and thumb, into the fire.

CURING A BURN.

To cure a burn, the following words were used—

> "Here come I to cure a burnt sore;
> If the dead knew what the living endure
> The burnt sore would burn no more."

The operator, after having repeated the above, blows his breath three times upon the burnt place. The above recipe was believed to have been communicated to a daughter who had been burned by the spirit of her deceased mother.

BELIEF REGARDING ELF SHOT.

It was fully believed in Shetland that when a cow was suddenly taken ill she was elf-shot—that is, that a particular kind of spirits called Trows, who are different in their nature from fairies, have discharged a stone arrow at her and wounded her with it. Though no wound could be discovered externally, there were different persons, both male and female, who pretended to feel it in the flesh, and to cure it by repeating certain words over the cow. They also folded a cinder in a leaf taken from a particular part of the psalm-book, and secured it in the hair of the cow. This was not only considered an infallible cure, but was believed to serve as a charm against future attacks.

WEARING CHARMS.

This practice was nearly allied to one

which was very prevalent, and of which some traces still exist in what would be esteemed a more enlightened part of the world, *i.e.*, wearing a small piece of the branch of the rowan tree wrapped around with red thread and sewed into some parts of the garments, to guard against the effects of the evil eye or witchcraft—

> " Rowan tree and red thread
> Will drive the witches a' wud."

SINGULAR CALVING CUSTOM.

When a cow calved it was the custom with some, as soon after as possible, to set a cat on the calf's neck and draw it along her back and then to seat it on the middle of the cow's back, draw it down the one side and pull it up the other, tail foremost. This ceremony was supposed to prevent the cow being carried away while in a weak state by the trows. This practice was styled, enclosing the cow in a magic circle.

THE DOINGS OF FAIRIES.

As the trows were said to have a remarkable relish for what was good in the way of eating or drinking, whenever a cow or sheep happened to turn sick or die it was firmly believed they had taken the real animal away and something of a trow breed substituted in its place. Those persons indulged with a glimpse of the interior of a trow's dwelling, asserted they had beheld their own cow led in to be slaughtered while at the same time their friends on the surface of the earth saw her fall by an invisible hand and tumble over a precipice.

Sometimes, also, the trows required a nurse for their children, they also having a time to be born and a time to die, and therefore females while engaged in nursing their own children required to be watched very narrowly lest they should be carried off to perform the office of wet nurse to some little trow, of gentle birth who had either lost its mother, or whose station amongst her own race exempted her from the drudgery of nursing her own offspring.

There is a place in Shetland called Trowland, a name which indicates the superstitious notions regarding it, as it signifies "the high land of the trows." The internal recesses of knolls were considered the favourite residences of the trows, and they were seldom passed without fear and awe by the primitive Shetlanders. And if after night-fall there was a necessity for passing that way, a live coal was carried to ward off their attacks.

NEIGHBOUR'S PROFITS.

In order that a person might take away and secure for herself the summer profits of her neighbour's cows, it was the practice to go clandestinely and pluck a handful of grass from the roof of the byre, and give it to her own cows, in the belief that the milk and butter which should have been her neighbour's would by this means become hers. In order to regain the profits thus transferred it was usual to milk privately a cow belonging to the person suspected of having taken them.

THE NEAGLE.

There was a trow called the neagle, somewhat akin to the water-kelpie of other lands, who made his appearance about mills, especially during grinding hours, in the shape of a beautiful pony. That he might attract the notice of the miller, he seized and held the wheel of the mill. Naturally, the miller went out to ascertain the cause of the stoppage, and, to his astonishment, a beautiful pony, saddled and bridled, stood ready to be mounted. If the miller should neglect warnings, and put his foot into the stirrup, his fate was sealed. Neither bit nor bridle availed him anything. Off went the pony, undeterred by bog or bank, and stinted not his course till in the deep sea he had thrown his venturesome rider, when he himself vanished in a flash of fire. Fortunately, however, most millers were proof against the temptation, and, instead of mounting the pony, saluted him on the nose with a fiery brand, which at once rid them of his presence.

CASTING THE HEART.

It was formerly believed that when an individual was attenuated by sickness, his heart was worn away or taken from him by some evil genii. A person skilled in casting the heart was at once sent for, who, with many mysterious ceremonies, melted lead and poured it through the bowl of a key or pair of scissors held over a sieve, which was also placed on a basin of cold water. The lead was melted and poured again and again till it assumed something like the form of a heart —at least the operator strove to persuade his patients and his friends that such was the case. This was hung suspended from the neck till the cure was completed.

CHAPTER XVIII.

Some old Highland customs—Courtship in former times—Marriage ceremonies—Manner of inviting guests—The bridegroom and the bride—The procession—Winning the kail—The Marriage feast—The dance—Funeral customs—Laying out the corpse—The lyke-wake—The coronach—The fiery cross—A Fasten's Eve custom—Some Lowland and general customs—Penal statutes at Galashiels—Peebles to the play—Marriage and kirking customs again—Family spirits or demons.

SOME OLD HIGHLAND CUSTOMS.

A HIGHLANDER used formerly never to begin anything of consequence on the day of the week on which the 3rd of May fell. This day was styled by them *La Sheachanna na bleanagh*, or the dismal day.

OLD COURTSHIP CUSTOMS.

The ancient courtship of the Highlanders had these curious customs attending it. After having privately obtained the consent of the fair one, the enamoured swain demanded her of her father. The lover and his friends assembled on a hill allotted for that purpose in every parish, and one of the latter was dispatched to obtain permission to wait upon the daughter. If he proved successful, he was again sent to invite the father and his friends to ascend the hill and partake of the contents of a whisky cask, which was never by any chance forgotten. The lover then advanced, took his father-in-law by the hand, and plighted his troth, whereupon the maiden was handed over to him.

OLD MARRIAGE CEREMONIES.

When a young couple proposed to get married, the nearest relations of both parties met to take the case into consideration. This ceremony, which was called the booking or contract, was generally ratified by no other ceremony than a few bottles of whisky. If the parties came to an understanding, the lovers were immediately declared bride and bridegroom, and some Tuesday or Thursday in the growth of the moon was fixed upon for the celebration of the nuptials. Meanwhile, to sustain the dignity of the bridal pair, from motives of policy as well as of state, they selected from their kinsmen two trustworthy persons each, who were delegated to the others—the male to protect the bride from being stolen (a practice once common), and the female to act as maid of honour.

A few days prior to the nuptial day the parties, with their attendants, perambulated the country inviting the guests, on which occasion they met with marked attention from old and young. The invitations were all delivered to the parties *in propria persona* at the fireside; and if the wedding was to be a cheap one, a small present was sometimes offered to and received by the bride. On the morning of the bridal day, some lady above the ordinary rank, who had been constituted mistress of the ceremonies for the day, arrived to deck the bride in her bridal attire, which was as splendid as ribbons and muslin could make it. The bridegroom was also provided with a decorator, who adorned him with marriage favours and other ornaments suited to the occasion.

Meanwhile volleys of musketry summoned the guests to the wedding. On their arrival they were invited into the breakfast apartment to partake of the prepared entertainment. Afterwards they repaired to the ballroom. Here the bride and bridegroom were seated at the upper end of the room, and received the company. The dancing and mirth were prolonged for some hours.

At the hour appointed the bridegroom selected a party of young men, who were despatched to summon the bride and her party to the marriage ceremony. Their approach was announced by volleys of musketry fired by some of the bride's men, most of the guests being furnished with pistols.

Then the bride and her maidens prepared themselves for the procession. The bride was mounted upon a steady horse, then drams went round to her health and happiness. The company being all in readiness, she left the home of her childhood amid the cheers of the assembled crowd. Marching to the inspiring sound of bagpipes and the discharge of musketry, the bride's party proceeded to the place appointed for the marriage. The bridegroom's followed at some little distance, and when both parties had arrived at the rendezvous, the bridegroom's party stood in the rear till the bride's party entered the meeting-house, she and her attendants having the precedence throughout the day.

During the marriage ceremony, great care was taken that no dogs passed between the bridal pair, and particular attention was paid to having the bridegroom's left shoe without buckle or latchet, in order to prevent witches from casting their unlucky spells over him and his bride. As soon as the nuptial knot was tied, the candidates for the honour of "winning the kail," as they styled it, drove off pell-mell, striving who was to be the lucky person. Both parties, now mingling together, proceeded with boisterous mirth to the bridegroom's house, the scene of the further festivities of the night.

A volley of fire-arms announced the approach of the couple, and soon the bride was assailed by her well-wishers with the bridal bread and cheese. The newly-married pair then seated themselves at the upper end of the principal banqueting table, and the guests were arranged according to their quality round the other and far-stretching tables. The attendants who waited upon the guests presented each with a spoon, which he was obliged carefully to return at the conclusion of the feast. The spoon was followed by the hardly-contested kail, &c. The dinner being over, the shemit reel was the next object of attention. All the company assembled on the lawn, with flambeaux, and formed into a circle. The bridal pair and their retainers then danced a sixsome reel, each putting a piece of silver into the musician's hand. Those wishing to do so, might then succeed and dance with the bride and the two maids of honour, and were rewarded both at the commencement and termination of each reel by the usual salutes. The shemit reel over, the guests re-occupied their seats in the original order, and dancing and mirth concluded the evening.

OLD FUNERAL CUSTOMS IN THE HIGHLANDS.

At a funeral, a fall sustained by one of the bearers of the body was considered ominous of the person's speedy death. It was also esteemed very unlucky to look at a person's funeral from the door of a house or from windows having a *stone lintel*. On the death of a Highlander, the corpse being stretched on a board covered with a linen wrapper, the friends laid on the breast of the deceased a wooden platter containing a small quantity of salt and earth, unmixed. The earth was meant as an emblem of the corruptible body, while the salt was an emblem of the immortal soul. All fire was extinguished where a corpse was kept, and it was accounted so ominous of evil for a dog or cat to pass over it that the poor creature was instantly deprived of life.

THE LYKE-WAKE.

This was a custom formerly celebrated at funerals. The evening after the death of any person, the relations and friends of the deceased met at the house, attended by bagpipes and fiddles. The nearest of kin, be it wife, son, or daughter, opened a melancholy ball, dancing and crying violently at the same time. This custom was derived from their northern ancestors. It continued till daybreak, and was attended with very unseemly gambols and frolics amongst the younger portion of the company. If the corpse remained unburied for two nights, the same rites were continued. In imitation of the Scythians, the Highlanders rejoiced at their friends' delivery from the misery of this world.

THE CORONACH.

The Coronach, or singing at funerals, is still kept up, to some extent, in some parts of the Highlands. The songs are generally in praise of the deceased, or a recital of the valiant deeds of his ancestors.

THE FIERY CROSS.

When a chieftain wished to summon his clan on any sudden or important emergency, he killed a goat, and, making a cross of light wood, burned its extremities in the fire, and then extinguished the flames in the animal's blood. This was called the Fiery Cross, also *Creau Toigh*, or the Cross of Shame, because disobedience to what the symbol implied inferred infamy. This cross was transferred from hand to hand, and sped through the chief's territories with incredible velocity. At sight of the Fiery Cross, every man from 16 to 60 was obliged to repair at once to the appointed place of meeting. He who neglected the summons exposed himself to the penalties of fire and sword, which were emblematically denoted by the bloody and burned marks, upon the fiery herald of woe.

A FASTEN'S EVE CUSTOM.

Fasten's Eve corresponded with Shrove Tuesday. The entertainment peculiar to this night was the matrimonial brose. This wholesome dish was generally made of the soup of a jigget of beef or mutton made into brose. Ere ever the soup was put into the plate, a ring was placed in the meal, which it was the aim of each partaker to get. Should any of the candidates for matrimony find the ring more than once, he might rest assured of his marrying before the next anniversary. The brose being despatched, the *Bannich Junit*, or Sauty Bannocks, were next produced.

PENAL STATUTES AT GALASHIELS.

Under the somewhat strange name of penal statutes, there existed in Galashiels the following kind and friendly old custom. The tenants of the barony—namely, the farmers—had, it seems, to pay a penny of fine at the bailie's court every time they "loupit" the laird's dykes. At Candlemas, when the tenantry dined at the tavern with the laird, the pence were regularly paid with the rents, and went towards the defraying of the reckoning.

PEEBLES TO THE PLAY.

The ancient and oft-referred-to town of Peebles is celebrated as being the scene of the quaint old poem, Christ's Kirk, ascribed to the royal poet, James I., and said to have been composed by him with a view to promote a love of archery among his subjects.

> " At Beltane quhen alle bodie boune
> To Peebles to the play
> To hear the singin and the soundis
> The solace suth to say.
>
> " Be firth and forrest furth they sound,
> They gray that them full gay,
> God wot that wold they do that stound,
> For it was their first day,
> They said,
> Of Peebles to the play."

In his poem the author represents a great annual festival of music, diversions, and feasting :—

> " Was never in Scotland heard nor sene
> Sic dancing and deray,
> Nowhir at Falkland on the green
> Nor Peebles at the play."

This festival, which was attended by all the inhabitants of the south of Scotland, arrayed in their best apparel, took place in May. The Beltane fires at Peebles must be considered as the representative of the ancient play. Till about the middle of last century the annual fair was distinguished by a horse race and other festivities approaching nearer to the character of the Play than the mere tryst to which it afterwards degenerated.

OTHER MARRIAGE AND KIRKING CUSTOMS.

To refer to marriage and kirking customs again. It was formerly the custom in many parts of Scotland for the bride, immediately after the wedding, to walk round the church unattended by the bridegroom. And matrimony was avoided in the months of January and May—

"If you are fond of proverbs always say,
No lass proves thrifty who is wed in May."

After baptism the first meat that the company tasted was *crowdie*, a mixture of meal and water, or meal and ale. Of this every person took three spoonfuls. The mother never set about any work till she had been kirked. In the Church of Scotland there is no ceremony observed on such occasions, but in this instance the woman, attended by some of her neighbours, entered the church, sometimes in service time, but often when it was empty, went out again, walked round it, and then returned home. It has happened that after baptism, the father placed a basket filled with bread and cheese on the pot-hook that hung suspended over the fire, in the middle of the room, in which the company were, and the child was handed across the fire, with the design to frustrate all attempts of evil spirits, or evil eyes. This custom seems to have been designed as a purification, and was of idolatrous origin, as the Israelites made their children to pass through the fire to Moloch.

FAMILY SPIRITS.

Almost every Highland and Lowland family possessing any claims to distinction had in former times its spirit or demon with its own peculiar attributes. Thus the family of Rothiemurchus had the *Bodach-an-dun*, or ghost of the hill; Kincardine's, the spectre of the bloody hand; Gartinberg House was haunted by *Bodach Garten*; Tulloch Gorm by *Mang Mulloch*, or the girl with the hairy left hand. The little spectres called *Tarans*, or the souls of unbaptised infants, were, it is said, often seen flitting among woods and secluded dells, lamenting in soft voices their hard fate. The Macleans of Lochbuy had their headless horseman, who has been heard in the silence of the night careering on horseback round the castle ringing his bridle-rein; the Ogilvies of Airlie, fairy music; Kincardine Castle had its lady in green, who sat weeping beneath a particular tree when the dark shadow of death hovered near the family of Graham; the house of Forbes of Balmano, their Lady Green Sleeves, and so on.

CHAPTER XIX.

Holding Kate Kennedy's Day at St. Andrews—Golf again—Amusing account of its origin and history—Holy well customs at Dunkeld—Holy wells at Huntly—Numerous holy wells over Scotland—Superstitious customs connected therewith—The burning of the Clavie at Burghead.

KATE KENNEDY'S DAY.

THE following celebration is observed annually by students at St. Andrews, attending the United College of St. Salvator and St. Leonard during the fourth year. Kate Kennedy's Day is yearly fixed by the observers for the last week in February or the beginning of March. The students meet at an appointed place at noon, when they array themselves in masquerade attire. They then form a procession. The leading performer, Kate Kennedy, is dressed in female garb, and mounted on horseback. Kate has a bodyguard, attended by a mounted escort. A drummer leads the way discoursing martial music. Each member of the procession represents some historical character, such as the Pope, the Stuart kings, Roman citizens, Greek Philosophers, etc. The cavalcade first proceeds to the college quadrangle, where Kate receives a congratulatory address. They then visit the private houses of the different professors, who are cheered or hooted according to the estimation in which they are held. The day's proceedings terminated in a banquet. Dr. Charles Rogers proceeds to say that the origin of this celebration is involved in some doubt. It seems to combine the honours paid in Romish times to the memory of St. Catherine, with a public recognition of the good services of the pious James Kennedy, Bishop of the See, who founded St. Salvator's College in 1455. A bell was placed in the college steeple by

Bishop Kennedy who dedicated it to St. Catherine. This was recast the third time in 1686, when a procession attended its suspension. Probably the modern observance began at this period.

GOLF AGAIN.

St. Andrews, as we have before stated, is the head-quarters of golf. A golfing society was established there in 1754, and two grand meetings of this club are held annually in May and October. The following amusing account of golfing at St. Andrews is taken, we believe, from the *Pall Mall Gazette*.

Here a man is playing golf all day long. He is scarcely ever in the house except when he is in bed and dreaming of 'bunkers' and 'hog-bucket-anes,' and the other mysteries of the game. How old golf is at St. Andrews no one knows. Probably when St. Regulus arrived here in 370 A.D., he found the natives absorbed in their pastime, and indifferent to religious matters. I daresay they howled out " Fore" at him, and took no other notice of him and his relics. In the fifteenth century golf was put down by Act of Parliament. The earliest document about golf I have been able to discover is on the seal of a Bishop of the twelfth century. The seal represents the tall square tower of St. Regulus as it still stands, and in the field are two golf clubs crossed in the form of a St. Andrew's Cross; at least if these objects are *not* golf clubs what are they? The game is as popular as ever here, and at once forces itself on the attention of the observer.

As you approach St. Andrews by railway the links are found in the possession of men in red coats equipped with *arma campestria* like the old Bishop of Galloway (1612) for whom the devil came in the very midst of a game of golf.—(See Proud's *History of the Kirk*). Men are not the only persons thus armed. Every lady who respects herself carries a " putter." Even infants in arms have little clubs in their hands. They suck the handles, I believe, and thus aid the process of teething. Every small boy has a club, with which he " addresses himself," to imaginary balls wherever he may be,—at home, in the drawing-room, or in the streets or gardens. The eternal swinging of clubs adds much to the misery of nervous persons at St. Andrews. He is not comforted either by the howls of

"Fore," (that is, being interpreted, "get out of the way, if you don't every bone in your body will be broken, confound you!") which greets him on all sides whenever he leaves his lodgings. After calling out "Fore," at St. Andrews, you may commit, I believe, any crime of assault and battery with the *arma campestria* without fear of the law of Scotland.

HOLY WELL CUSTOM AT DUNKELD.

The Grenge Well, Dunkeld, is still to some extent sought after by people who come even from a distance bringing their sick children in order that these may drink of the life-giving water, and be healed of their various ailments. Silver coins have occasionally been thrown into the water in return for supposed favours received; and rags and scraps of the sick persons clothes are left lying around, as offerings to the guardian spirit of this much esteemed spot.

HOLY WELLS OVER SCOTLAND.

St. Mungo's Well in Huntly, St. Fergon's Well near Inverlochy, the well at Metheshirin near Dufftown, the well of Moulblairie in Banffshire, St. Colman's Well in the parish of Kilbarn, in Ross-shire, Culboakie, also in

Ross-shire, St. Mary's Well in the birch wood above Culloden House, the Craigie Well in the Black Isles opposite Inverness, the Wallack Well, and the Corsmall Well, at Glass in Banffshire, together with "these superstitious round-earth wells of Menteith," are still resorted to by the common people. Miss Gordon Cumming tells us, that among the various efforts made to check the favourite well worship two centuries ago, was an order from the Privy Council appointing commissioners to wait at Christ's Well in Menteith on the 1st May, and to seize all who might assemble at the spring, and imprison them in Doune Castle.

CURIOUS OLD CUSTOM AT BURGHEAD.

According to Miss Gordon Cumming, from time immemorial the fisher folk and seamen of Burghead, have on Yule night, O. S., met at the west end of the town carrying an old barrel and other combustible materials. This barrel having been sawn in two, the lower half is nailed into a long spoke of firewood which serves for a handle. *This nail must not be struck by a hammer* but driven in with a stone. The half barrel is then filled with dry wood saturated with tar, and built up like a pyramid, leaving only a hollow to receive a burning peat, *for no lucifer match must be applied.* A fresh libation of tar completes the Clavie, which is shouldered by one of the lads, quite regardless of the streams of burning tar which of course trickle down his back. Should the bearer stumble or fall, the consequences would be unlucky indeed to the town and to himself. When weary of his burden a second is ready to fill the honoured post, and then a third and a fourth, till the Clavie has made a circuit of the town, when it is carried to a hillock called the Doorie, where a hollowed stone receives the fire spoke. Fresh fuel is added, and in olden times the blaze continued all night and at length was allowed to burn itself out untouched. Now after a short interval the Clavie is thrown down the western side of the hill, and a desperate scramble ensues for the burning brands possession of which is accounted to bring good luck, and the embers are carried home and carefully preserved till the following year, as a safeguard against all manner of evil. In bygone times it was thought necessary that one man should carry it right round the town so the strongest was selected for this purpose.

Moreover it was customary to carry the Clavie round every ship in the harbour, a part of the ceremony which has latterly been discontinued. In 1875, however the Clavie was duly carried to one vessel just ready for sea. Handfuls of grain were thrown upon her deck, and amid a shower of fire-water she received the suggestive name of Doorie.—The modern part of the town is not included in the circuit. The meaning and origin of this custom are alike unknown.

CHAPTER XX.

Description of some of the old Druidical customs and their remains—The Ancient Gods of the Britains—The manner of celebrating the Bel-tein—The first day in May—The Relics of Druidical worship in Kincardineshire—The day of Baal's fire—The day of the Fire of Peace—Druidical Sacrifices—May and Hallowe'en observances of Druidical origin—Tinto Hill in Lanarkshire—Remains of Druidical customs at Mouline—In Perthshire—At Cambuslang—Passing children and cattle through the fire.

REFERENCE has been made to the Beltane customs. The once general observances of Beltane or Beltein (the 1st day of May), now rank amongst the things of the past. In former times this festival was observed both in the Highlands and Lowlands of Scotland, and dedicated to certain mystic observances connected chiefly with fire and the partaking of certain dishes, such as a particular caudle, some of which was afterwards spilled on the ground by way of libation, a relic no doubt of the more ancient libations to such heathen deities as Odin and Thor. One of the ancient gods of the Britains was Belus or Belinus, identical it is believed with the Assyrian god Bel or Belus; and in all probability from this Pagan deity, comes the Scots term of Beltis, or the 1st day of May. The origin of this once favourite festival is supposed to date from the Druids, who in these isles extinguished all the fires in the district until the tithes were paid. On repayment of these the household fires were re-kindled.

BELTANE CUSTOMS.

On the 1st of May, the herdsmen of every village used formerly to hold their Bel-tein or usual sacrifice, as follows:—They cut a square trench on the ground, leaving the turf in the middle; on that they made a fire of wood, on which they dressed a caudle of eggs, butter, oatmeal, and milk. Each of the company brought besides the ingredients for making the caudle, plenty of beer and whisky. The rites begun with spilling some of the caudle on the ground by way of libation. That done, every one took a cake of oatmeal upon which were raised knobs, each dedicated to some particular being, the supposed preserver of their flocks and herds, or to some animal, the real destroyer of them. Each person then turned his face to the fire, broke off a knob, and throwing it over his left shoulder, said, " This I give to thee ; preserve thou my horses ; this to thee, preserve thou my sheep," and so on. After this, they used the same ceremony to the noxious animals. " This I give to thee, O fox ; spare thou my lambs ; this to thee, O hooded crow ; this to thee, O eagle." When the ceremony was over they dined on the caudle ; and after the feast was finished, what was left was carefully hidden away by two persons deputed for that purpose ; but on the following Sunday the herdsmen re-assembled, and finished the remains of the former feast.

On New Year's day the Highlanders burned juniper before their cattle. A cross was cut on some sticks which were dipped in pottage, and the Thursday before Easter, each of these was placed over the sheep cot, the stable, or the cow-house. On the first of May, these were carried to the hill where the accustomed rites were celebrated, and on the conclusion of the feast they were replaced in their former positions. This custom was originally styled *Clou in Beltein*, or the split fire of the branch of the rock.

On the summit of the hill of Garnock in Kincardineshire, there are two large cairns, the relics of Druidism, about a mile asunder. The larger is fifty yards in diameter, and must have been a superb structure in its day. It had been carefully surrounded by a ring of large blocks of freestone. On these the Druidical or heathen priests are supposed to have lighted great fires at certain seasons of the year in honour of their god Bel, the sun, the same as the Scripture Baal. These fires were lighted and assemblies held at the cairns both for religious and judicial purposes. The fires were supposed to be lighted particularly on their two great festivals. The first was termed in Gaelic, La Beiltin, the day of Beil's fire, *i.e.*, the 1st of May, the beginning of their year, when great rejoicings were held for the return of the new year. Among other ceremonies, putting part of a mixture of meal, milk, and eggs, etc., on a piece of bread, they throw it over the left shoulder, saying each time, " This is to you, O mists and storms, spare our pastures and our corn ; this to you, O eagle, spare our lambs and our kids; this is to thee, O fox and falcon, spare our poultry."

The second was La Samhin, the day of the fire of peace, *i.e.*, the 1st of November. This was the most solemn of all their festivals, when the Druids, it is supposed, meet at the centre cairn to hold rejoicings for finishing the harvest, and to maintain the peace by adjusting every dispute, and deciding every controversy. Then too, all were obliged to extinguish their fires on the preceding evening, and come for a supply of the consecrated fire on the cairns. But of this, no person could obtain any share till he had made every reparation required by the priests. If he was refractory, the sentence of excommunication was pronounced against him, and this was worse far than death. None durst afford him shelter, or fire or food, or any office of humanity, under pain of the same sentence being passed upon themselves.

On these two occasions the Druids offered bloody sacrifices, and their victims consisted not only of beasts but of men. Two fires being kindled, Toland tells us, that the men and beasts to be sacrificed, were made to pass between these fires by way of consecration. Hence the Gaelic proverb, *Edin-da-hin-Veaul*, " the jeopardy of Baal," or between Baal's two fires, the most dreadful danger from which escape would be miraculous.

In Lanarkshire there is a hill called Tinto, which name denotes the hill of fire, its summit having been in early times either used as an observatory or a place of worship where Druidical rites were performed at the Beltane and other festivals. The Beltane, or rural festival on the 1st of May, was long observed in the parish of Mouline. Hallowe'en was kept sacred. As soon as it was dark, a person set fire to a brush or broom, fastened round a pole, and attended by a crowd, ran through the village. He then flung it on the ground and heaped large quantities of combustibles upon it and made a fine blaze. A whole tract when thus illuminated presented a grave spectacle. Formerly the people used to dance and sing round these fires, which were frequently surrounded by circular trenches symbolical of the sun. In Perthshire the fires are still kept up. In some instances when the bonfire begins to burn low, a circle of stones is placed round it, one of which represents each individual present. Should any of these be moved from its original position before next morning, it betokens speedy death to that person. Dechmont Hill, situated in the parish of Cambuslang, was a place where our forefathers lighted the Beltane. In the Statistical Account of Scotland (1848) it is stated that a thick stratum of charcoal was discovered underneath a structure of fine loam on the summit of the hill. When the country people saw it they expressed no surprise, as the tradition was familiar to them that it was here where the former inhabitants of the country had been in the habit of lighting their Beltane.

Tulliebeltane, in Perthshire, signifies the eminence, or rising ground of the fire of Belus.

In the neighbourhood is a Druidical temple of eight upright stones, where it is supposed the fire was formerly kindled. There is also a small temple of the same kind, and in its neighbourhood a well, which is still an object of veneration with the people, who assemble here on Beltane morning to drink of the water and then encircle it nine times. Afterwards in like manner they go round the temple.

In some parts of the Highlands children still roll bannocks down the hill sides to learn their future fate, which cakes on Beltane eve anxious mothers carefully baked. The cakes are flat and round, having on one side the cross, the sign of life; on the other the cipher, signifying death. Next morning the children assemble on a neighbouring height, place their fateful bannocks in a line, and send them down the slope edge-ways. This is done three times, and should the cross turn up most frequently when the cakes arrive at the foot of the hill, then the owner will live to see another Beltane; but if, on the other hand, the cipher appears, death is to be his portion before the next annual festival.

The custom of passing children and cattle

through the fire was long in force in the Western Islands. At the great fire festivals in the Highlands and in Ireland, fathers took their children in their arms and leapt thrice through the flames. Even in the beginning of this century it was customary in some of the more remote districts of the Highlands for the young of both sexes to meet on the moors on the first of May, and, after cutting a round table in the green sward with a trench round it sufficiently large to admit of their encircling it, they kindled a fire in the middle and prepared a mess of eggs and milk, of which all partook.

They then baked oat-cakes, a piece for each present, and one which was burned black. These cakes were afterwards shuffled in a man's bonnet, and each person blindfolded drew one. Whoever got the black piece had to leap thrice through the flames. The original meaning of this probably was that he became a sacrifice to Baal, and doubtless in old days was actually offered up,—the object of this ceremony being to propitiate the sun-god, and thus secure a good harvest.

In some parts of Perthshire it is still the custom for the cow-herd of the village to go from house to house on May morning, collecting fresh eggs and meal, and then lead the way to some hill top, where a hole is dug and a fire lighted therein; then lots are cast, and he on whom the lot falls must leap seven times over the fire while the young folks dance round in a circle; then they cook their eggs and cakes, and all sit down and partake thereof. In Scotland the Midsummer's Eve Festival was observed till very recent times. It was customary to kindle great bonfires near the corn fields with burning torches to secure a blessing on their crops.

THE END.

www.ingramcontent.com/pod-product-compliance
Lightning Source LLC
Chambersburg PA
CBHW021812230426
43669CB00008B/730